The

Investor's Guide

To

Cannabis Stocks

Dr. James V. Baker

Copyright © 2021 James V Baker

All rights reserved.

ISBN: 9798546319304

THE AUTHOR

Dr. James V. Baker enjoyed a successful and varied career as an author, commercial banker, investment banker, city treasurer, investment adviser, NASD arbitrator, consultant, tenured university professor, and tennis professional. His academic credentials include having earned a master degree in Economics and a doctorate degree majoring in Finance both from Florida State University.

A Chair of Banking was established by the Oklahoma Bankers Association for him to occupy at the University of Oklahoma in the College of Business. Baker was Chairman of the American Bankers Association (ABA) Commercial Lending and Graduate Commercial Lending schools. He was also Chairman of the ABA Certified Commercial Lender accreditation board. He has trained thousands of commercial lenders and bank examiners.

Dr. Baker is known as the father of Asset/Liability Management (ALM) and wrote the original book on it for the ABA. It out sold any previous banking book the ABA ever published. It was translated into Japanese and also set sales records in Japan.

His ALM theory revolutionized financial risk management and became generally accepted worldwide. The methodological approach introduced in his book has been implemented far beyond the banking industry.

Baker was also Chairman of the Oklahoma Development Authority and under his leadership the authority financed billions of dollars in economic development. He was also President of the Economic Club of Oklahoma.

In 1979 he founded James Baker and Company, which is now known as The Baker Group. It is an investment bank with offices throughout the USA. It is one of the nation's largest independently owned securities firms specializing in investment portfolio and interest rate risk management for community financial institutions.

In the 1980s Baker had his own family of mutual funds. He liquidated 100% of the stocks in his equity fund two days before the crash of October 1987 and his fund was the only mutual fund to report its net asset value (NAV) rose on the day the market crashed.

DISCLAIMER

Dr. Baker is not a registered investment adviser or a broker/dealer. All investment and financial opinions expressed in this book are from personal research and experience and intended solely for educational purposes. Although best efforts have been made to ensure that all information is accurate, occasionally unintended errors and misprints may occur.

CONTENTS

THE AUTHOR ii
DISCLAIMER iii
EXHIBITS viii
PREFACE x
INTRODUCTION xi
CHAPTER 1 1
EMERGENCE OF PUBLICLY HELD CANNABIS COMPANIES 1
- GW Pharma Breaks Through with Epidiolex 1
- Cannabis Based Drugs 2
- GW Pharma Financials 2
- Jazz GW Pharma Transaction Metrics 3
- Canada Gives Birth to The Cannabis Industry 3
- The Lure of Great Wealth 4
- Reality Begins 5
- Hallucinogenic Accounting 5
- Five Companies Dominate Canada 6
- Canopy Growth Corporation 6
- Constellation Brands 8
- Canopy Financials 9
- Tilray 10
- Tilray IPO 11
- Tilray Deals 13
- Tilray Financials 13
- Aphria 15
- Aphria Financials 17
- Tilray Aphria Merger 18
- Aurora Cannabis Inc 18
- Aurora Financials 19
- Cronos 21
- Cronos Financials 21
- Summary 22

CHAPTER 2 24
VERTICALLY INTEGRATED U.S. MARIJUANA COMPANIES 24

- Entrepreneurs 25
- A Need to Go Public 26
- Economies of Scale 26
- The U.S. Multi-State Operator (MSO) Model 27
- Cannabis Company Balance Sheet Analysis 28
- iAnthus Situation 28
- Income Taxes Payable 29
- Current Portion of Debt Payable 30
- Current Lease Liabilities 31
- Accumulated Deficit 31
- Intangible Assets and Goodwill 32
- Impairment Charge Threat 34
- Tangible Equity Capital 34
- Cannabis Company Income Statement Analysis 35
- Importance of Margin 37
- Margin Analysis of U.S. Cannabis Companies 37
- Gross Profit Margin 37
- Operating Expense Ratio 38
- Net Operating Margin 39
- Margin Analysis of Canada's Big Five 39
- Cannabis Company Profitability 40
- Cannabis Company Cash Flow Analysis 40
- Non-GAAP and Non-IFRS Measures 47
- History of EBITDA 47
- Evolution of Adjusted EBITDA 50
- Calculation of Adjusted EBITDA by Cannabis Companies 52
- Main Ingredients of Adjusted EBITDA 56
- Interest 56
- Taxes 58
- Share-Based Compensation 58
- Adjusted EBITDA Margin 60

- Summary 60

CHAPTER 3 62

PROVIDERS OF ANCILLARY PRODUCTS AND SERVICES 62

- Innovative Industrial Properties, Inc. 63
- GrowGeneration 65
- Scotts Miracle-Gro 66
- Jazz Pharmaceuticals 67
- Hydrofarm Holdings 67
- Greenlane Holdings, Inc. 68
- KushCo Holdings, Inc. 69
- Greenlane Holdings and KushCo Merger 69
- Summary 70

CHAPTER 4 71

OTHER CANNABIS INVESTMENT VEHICLES 71

- Exchange Traded Funds – ETFs 71
- ETF Advantages 72
- Cannabis ETFs 73
- ETF Managers Group Cannabis ETFs 74
- AdvisorShares Cannabis ETFs 75
- Other Cannabis ETFs 78
- Special Purpose Acquisition Company (SPAC) 78
- Cannabis SPAC 79
- Cannabis Strategies Acquisition Corporation 79
- SPAC Issue Similarities 81
- The Cannabis SPAC Universe 81
- Stable Road Acquisition Corporation 83
- Summary 84

CHAPTER 5 85

CHEAPEST TO MOST EXPENSIVE CANNABIS STOCKS 85

- The Problem Valuing Cannabis Company Stocks 85
- Valuation Metrics 86
- Operating Cash Flow Valuation Metric 87
- Tax Adjusted Operating Cash Flow Valuation Metric 89

- **Net Income After Taxes Per Share – PE Ratio Valuation Metric** 90
- **PEG Ratio Valuation Metric** 91
- **Fixation on Growth** 94
- **Accretion and Dilution** 98
- **Book Value Valuation Metric** 100
- **Tangible Book Value Valuation Metric** 102
- **Adjusted Operating Income Valuation Metric** 103
- **Adjusted EBITDA Valuation Metric** 104
- **Total Revenue Valuation Metric** 105
- **Large Canadian LP Stock Valuation Metrics** 106
- **Providers of Ancillary Products and Services Valuation Metrics** 107
- **Summary** 108

CHAPTER 6 109

EPILOGUE 109

APPENDIX A 112

PUBLICLY HELD CANNABIS COMPANIES 112

APPENDIX B 136

GLOSSARY 136

APPENDIX C 139

BIBLIOGRAPHY 139

EXHIBITS

2.1	Marijuana Legal Status by State as of June 1, 2021	25
2.2	Adequacy of U.S. Cannabis Company Cash Positions: December 31, 2020	29
2.3	Accumulated Deficit and Financial Leverage: December 31, 2020	33
2.4	Trulieve Cannabis Corporation Statement of Operations and Income: 2020	36
2.5	U.S. Company Operating Margins: 2020	38
2.6	Canadian Company Operating Margins: 2020	39
2.7	Ayr Wellness Statements of Cash Flows for 2020	41
2.8	Company Free Cash Flow for 2020	43
2.9	CAPEX Relative to Depreciation: 2020	49
2.10	Trulieve Performance Measures: 2018-2021	52
2.11	Cannabis Adjusted EBITDA Items Listing	54
2.12	Interest, Taxes, Share-Based Compensation and Adjusted EBITDA for 2020	57
3.1	Innovative Industrial Properties Results: 2018-2020	64
3.2	GrowGeneration Results: 2018-2020	65
4.1	Cannabis ETFs	74
4.2	MJ Top 10 Holdings: July 9, 2021	75
4.3	AdvisorShares Top 10 Holdings in MSOS and YOLO: July 9, 2021	77
4.4	U.S. SPAC IPOs: 2016-2021	79
4.5	Cannabis SPACs: 2017-Mid 2021	82
5.1	Valuation Metrics of Vertically Integrated Cannabis Companies for 2020	88
5.2	Share Price to Net Operating Cash Flow: 2020	89
5.3	Price Earnings (PE) Multiple: 2020	92
5.4	PEG Multiple: 2020	93
5.5	Cannabis Company Shares Outstanding: 2019 and 2010	97

5.6   Shares Outstanding: 2019 and 2020...99

5.7   Book Value Multiples..101

5.8   Revenue Multiples..106

5.9   Valuation Metrics for Top 5 Canadian Licensed Producers for 2020................107

5.10 Valuation Metrics of Providers of Ancillary Products/Services for 2020...........108

PREFACE

During the past four years Seeking Alpha has published more than 40 articles and hundreds of comments I have written about publicly held cannabis stocks. Those articles brought forth a wealth of comments and questions from readers. One of my articles, "Cannabis Stocks Ranked from Cheapest to Most Expensive," became possibly the most read cannabis article ever written on cannabis stocks It was published on October 1, 2020; and, in a rarity for articles, it still attracts new readers on a daily basis almost a year after its publication.

I started to update that article to incorporate many new ideas along with comments and suggestions made by readers. I soon realized however the article was way too lengthy. When I mentioned that to a few followers they suggested I write a book on investing in cannabis stocks.

I have been investing in the cannabis sector since 2014, so I have witnessed the birthing pains of a new industry from a front-row seat. In that process, I have gone through stages of investor elation, as well as grief, and managed to emerge with an acceptable amount of scar tissue and significant profits. Importantly, however, I have been able to identify financial metrics of successful and unsuccessful cannabis companies. This book reveals those metrics and applies them to publicly traded cannabis stocks.

As such, this book focuses on the financial fundamentals of a cannabis company that underpin its stock price. I personally appreciate and use technical analysis in arriving at investment decisions, however, chart patterns are ignored in this book.

Traditional fundamental and technical analyses are as applicable to selecting cannabis stocks as stocks in any other sector. Investments made with the rigorous application of fundamental and technical analysis do not guarantee success, but they do tip the scales in the favor of investors who use these techniques just like card counting raises a blackjack player's odds of winning.

Company stock prices get divorced from company fundamentals and technical for periods of time, and they may get alarmingly overvalued or horribly undervalued. To paraphrase John Maynard Keynes, it is wise to remember that a stock price can remain irrational longer than an investor can remain solvent.

After reading this book, you will be armed with a wealth of knowledge that should enable you to profitably invest in cannabis companies. You may even find financial metrics presented in this book to be helpful in analyzing stocks in other sectors.

INTRODUCTION

This book begins by discussing the first cannabis companies that issued shares traded on organized stock exchanges. These publicly held companies were foreign corporations, but their shares were bought by Unites States investors. The early companies introduced forms of corporate ownership that provided a template for others to follow. They also elevated the role of investor relations along with the use of social and traditional media.

Importantly, these companies established a pattern of financial reporting that diminished traditional measures of company performance. Instead, they presented measures of financial performance that purportedly provided a better picture of company operations.

The first cannabis companies to attract widespread investor attention were Canadian. The pathway they established to corporate formation was followed by hundreds of other cannabis companies. Most U.S. cannabis companies owe their corporate existence to the route taken by the earliest Canadian companies.

After discussing the important role played by the early publicly held cannabis companies, this book focuses on the United States cannabis industry and publicly traded companies with annual revenue of at least $25 million. A conscious attempt has been made to identify all companies meeting this criterion, but it is likely some have been accidentally overlooked.

For expository purposes Cannabis stocks are divided into three different categories: (1) shares of fully integrated pure cannabis companies; (2) shares of companies that provide products and services to cannabis companies; and (3) shares of exchange traded funds (ETF) that concentrate their investments in the cannabis sector. Fully integrated cannabis companies obtain 100% of their revenue from the sale of cannabis products. They cultivate, process, and distribute cannabis products.

Companies that provide products and services may obtain less than 100% of their revenue from the cannabis sector. These companies generally do not touch the plant, and, because of that, their shares can be listed on the NYSE and NASDAQ. Companies in this category are frequently viewed as the modern-day equivalent of the purveyors of picks and shovels to miners in the 1849 California gold rush.

Cannabis ETFs are actively managed by portfolio managers who invest in a portfolio of cannabis stocks. An ETF trades throughout the day just like any other stock. At the end of each trading day the net asset value (NAV) per share of an ETF is calculated just like a mutual fund.

An ETF can trade at a discount or premium to its NAV, but they are designed to minimize the size of any divergence by allowing market makers, large investors, and institutions to buy and sell large blocks of shares at the NAV. The relative attractiveness of cannabis company shares is identified by measuring actual company performance using generally accepted valuation metrics. The valuation metrics divided into balance sheet, profitability, and cash flow measures and by necessity are snapshots of actual recorded results as of a moment in time. A series of snapshots or observations would allow some forecasting; however, the companies have not been in existence long enough to make statistically significant forecasts.

Financial strengths and weaknesses of individual companies are identified. Individual companies are then compared to identify relative values. Furthermore, the cannabis sector is compared to a number of well-known companies in other economic sectors to gauge the relative value of the cannabis sector.

This book was written when the most recent audited data available were for the fiscal year ended December 31, 2020. The most recent interim, unaudited data were for the quarter ended March 31, 2021. All data were obtained directly SEC and SEDAR filings.

CHAPTER 1

EMERGENCE OF PUBLICLY HELD CANNABIS COMPANIES

The first publicly held cannabis company was GW Pharmaceuticals (GWPH), a British biopharmaceutical company started by Doctors Geoffrey Guy and Brian Whittle. In 1998 they obtained a cultivation license from the United Kingdom Home Office and the Medicines and Healthcare Regulatory Agency to grow cannabis from seeds and clones so they could conduct scientific research concerning the medicinal uses of the plant. GW Pharmaceuticals was initially listed on the AIM, the junior market of the London Stock Exchange in 2001. GW Pharma shares became listed in 2013 on the NASDAQ via American Depositary Receipts "ADRs" with one share of GWPH equaling 12 ordinary shares.

GWPH's first commercial product, Nabiximols (trade name Sativex) was approved in the UK in 2010 as a treatment for multiple sclerosis patients to alleviate neuropathic pain, spasticity, overactive bladder and other symptoms. In 2011 GWPH established a partnership with Bayer for the distribution of Sativex in the UK and has annually produced about 100 tons of it since 2012. Nabiximols is synthesized from two proprietary cannabis strains and is extracted with ethanol and carbon dioxide. Sativex is currently used to treat spasticity (muscle spasms and stiffness) caused by multiple sclerosis. The drug, delivered through a vaporizer, is approved in 25 countries but isn't available in the United States. GW Pharmaceuticals is, however, engaged in Phase 3 clinical trials that could soon lead to FDA approval of Sativex.

GW Pharma Breaks Through with Epidiolex

In 2015 GWPH initiated Phase 3 clinical trials of cannabidiol by mouth for treatment of two orphan conditions in children, Dravet and Lennox-Gastaut syndromes. GWPH also received fast track designation from the FDA for use of the drug candidate to treat newborns with epilepsy. The drug, under the brand name Epidiolex, was given FDA approval in June 2018 after pivotal Phase 3 trials with 516 patients were completed.

On September 27, 2018 the Drug Enforcement Agency "DEA" ruled Epidiolex would not face the same federal restrictions as other products made from marijuana. That made Epidiolex the first medication derived from marijuana that doctors could legally prescribe everywhere in the country.

The DEA decision applied only to Epidiolex; therefore, the flood gates were not opened for CBD based drugs from other pharmaceutical companies. To emphasize that point, the DEA stated in its Epidiolex announcement that it still considered CBD or cannabidiol in other forms to be a Schedule I drug just like heroin and LSD. Epidiolex is manufactured in England and shipped to and distributed by Greenwich Biosciences a U.S. subsidiary of GWPH. It began being dispensed as a CBD-infused strawberry syrup in November 2018.

GW Pharmaceuticals received marketing authorization for Epidiolex from the European Medicines Agency on September 23, 2019. The trade name for Epidiolex in Europe is Epidyolex. The CBD-based medicine was green lighted in Europe also for the treatment of Lennox-Gastaut syndrome (LGS) or Dravet syndrome in conjunction with clobazam.

Cannabis Based Drugs

In the past 40 years there have only been five-cannabis based drugs, including Epidiolex, introduced in the worldwide pharmaceutical market. Cesamet, a Valeant Pharmaceutical drug, was introduced in Canada in 1982 and in the US in 2006; Marinol, an Abbvie drug, was introduced in the US in 1986; Sativex, a GWPH drug, was introduced in Canada in 2005; and Syndros, an INSYS Therapeutics drug, was introduced in 2017. The four drugs introduced prior to Epidiolex are all synthetic products. It is significant that Epidiolex was the first plant-based cannabinoid to be approved by the FDA.

GW Pharma Financials

An historical analysis of financial statements of GWPH highlights the difficulties that await those cannabis companies planning to get rich by establishing or acquiring pharmaceutical companies to develop Cannabis based drugs. GWPH scientists engaged in pure research of cannabis for the sole purpose of discovering Cannabis based drugs for 23+ years and during that time the company never earned an operating profit or had positive operating free cash flow.

GW Pharma's journey to cannabis based pharmaceutical riches has been a rocky one. In fact, as of the end of its 2020 GWPH showed accumulated losses of $950 million, meaning that GWPH lost that amount of money during the first 22 years of its existence! In 2018 it only had $12.7 million in revenue and reported a net loss of $295 million or $10.61 per share. Thanks to the drug approvals, revenue jumped to $311.3 million in 2019 and to $527.2 million in 2020. It still, however, reported losses of $9 million in 2019 and $58.2 million in 2020. Despite the surge in sales, it continued to have negative cash flow from operations of $123 million in 2019 and $27.4 million in 2020.

Despite its continued losses and negative cash flow, investors did not abandon GW Pharma. In fact, it was always considered the leading medical marijuana, pharmaceutical company in the world. The public perception of GWPH as the leading company contributed to it always having a seemingly unjustifiable valuation, which became justified when Jazz Pharmaceuticals acquired GW Pharma on May 5, 2021.

Jazz GW Pharma Transaction Metrics

On February 3, 2021 Jazz announced it agreed to acquire 100% of GW Pharma for $200 cash and $20 in stock for every share of GWPH. Each share of GWPH, which was an ADR, equaled 12 ordinary shares of GW Pharma. Those amounts gave the transaction a total value of $7.2 billion. The $220 per share sale price represented a premium of 50% over the $146.25 closing price of GWPH the day prior to the announcement.

The sale price was 9.7 times book value and 9.9 times tangible book value at the end of 2020. The $7.2 billion was also 13.7 times GW Pharma's total revenue for 2020. Its total revenue had increased 69.3% from its 2019 revenue. Metrics such as sale price relative to cash flow, net income, and EBITDA could not be calculated since GW Pharma had a net loss, negative cash flow, and negative EBITDA in 2020.

Prior to the acquisition Jazz was much larger that GW Pharma. For example, Jazz total revenue in 2020 was $2.4 billion, which was 4.5 times larger than GW Pharma's revenue, such that GW Pharma's revenue would amount to only about 18% of total Jazz sales on a pro forma basis. Jazz equity capital of $3.7 billion was 5 times that of GW Pharma at the time of the transaction.

Canada Gives Birth to The Cannabis Industry

Canada became the unofficial birthplace of publicly held cannabis companies in April 2014 when Health Canada implemented Marijuana for Medical Purposes Regulations (MMPR). Its position was solidified on October 17, 2018 when Canada became the first developed nation to fully legalize marijuana. A less developed nation, Uruguay, had legalized it in 2013.

Like previous discoveries of uranium, gold, silver, oil, and natural gas, the emergence of cannabis created a frenzy of speculative activity that is uniquely Canadian. Entrepreneurs seeking the latest wealth generating vehicle quickly followed the well-trodden route made by prior generations and formed public companies by issuing stock on securities exchanges that were happy to get listing fees and capitalize on this newest sector of the Canadian economy.

Cannabis fever swept the nation as thousands of applicants sought governmental approval to obtain licensed producer (LP) status. At the same time, hundreds of companies were formed to issue stock on the exchanges to obtain funds to execute the dreams of their organizers. The fact that most of these people knew nothing about cultivating, processing and distributing marijuana was not as important as getting in on the action.

Today's publicly held Cannabis companies owe their existence to that cauldron of human activity designed to capitalize on the latest, greatest way to make a fortune in Canada. The organizers just copied the game plan used by mining companies that have long since disappeared. In fact, a significant number of the today's publicly traded cannabis companies went public via a reverse takeover (RTO) technique using the carcass of long dead mining companies.

As of June 22, 2021 there were 235 "Life Sciences" listings on the Canadian Securities Exchange (CSE) and most of those are cannabis companies. The CSE touts itself as "The Exchange for Entrepreneurs." At the present time there are 447 other listings of the CSE including 204 mining companies and 13 oil and gas companies. Many of the stocks on the CSE trade for pennies and are known as "penny stocks." Most brokerage firms and experienced investors recognize penny stocks are thinly traded, very volatile and easily manipulated, so they avoid them.

Other than the game plan on how to incorporate a company and do an IPO on a Canadian stock exchange, most of the organizers of these public cannabis companies knew nothing about operating a business. Many early entrants are already gone, but some have been able to survive. The survivors have all been able to replenish lost early investor cash with cash from new investors in a legal Ponzi-like fashion where investors are looking to "strike it rich."

The Lure of Great Wealth

The attribute that encouraged people to get involved in Canadian cannabis stocks was a deeply held conviction that great wealth was within reach. The prevailing belief was that the Canadian marijuana industry was in its infancy as shown by the fact that the number medical marijuana users registered with Health Canada was 28,115 in 2012; 60,000 in 2014; 220,000 in 2017; and 331,000 in 2018. Simple extrapolation of that trend suggested that there would be millions of users within a few years.

The media fanned the cannabis movement by chronicling the fortunes being made in Canada's newest industry. Reports of success lured people from all walks of life who believed they were getting in early. Just as a prior generation of Canadian investors had been lured by the glimmer of gold, cannabis investors saw marijuana as their ticket to vast riches.

These investors were especially excited, since the conventional wisdom was that legalization of recreational marijuana would open up the money faucet.

There was and still is a belief that the marijuana industry will at some time in the future rival the soft drink, candy, pharmaceutical, health food and other consumer packaged goods (CPG) industries in sales. The fervor about marijuana's future and Canada's unique positioning made it easy for Canadian cannabis companies to raise money.

It would be a huge understatement to say that Canadian cannabis companies became proficient at raising money. It would be more accurate to say that Canadian cannabis companies are the Olympic Gold Medalists of raising money. The amount of money raised was C$148 million in 2014, C$908 million in 2015, C$1.299 billion in 2016, C$3.530

billion in 2017, and C$13.792 billion in 2018. A total of C$19.677 billion was therefore raised in the first five years of publicly held cannabis company formation.

Once the lure of great wealth becomes embedded in the human mind, it does not take much to separate people from their money. Billions of dollars were raised by Canadian cannabis companies that continually lost money. The negative operating free cash flows that have characterized the Canadian cannabis sector since its inception keep getting funded by issuance of additional stock and/or debt instruments to investors captivated by dreams of great wealth.

Reality Begins

As publicly held Canadian cannabis companies evolved, their managements concluded that Canada's population of 36 million was insufficient to justify Cannabis company valuations even with the legalization of recreational marijuana. Once that insight dawned in Canadian cannabis company executive suites and board rooms, the bigger companies started gobbling up other domestic companies in a drive to capture market share and become vertically and horizontally integrated. The heightened M&A activity was accompanied by a desire to expand internationally. Accordingly, Canadian companies spent billions in Germany, Norway, Mexico, Jamaica, Argentina, Columbia, Uruguay, Portugal, Australia, and elsewhere. The drive to continually add more and more square feet of cultivation was especially notable, because there was a strongly held belief that there would be a shortage once the ban on recreational marijuana consumption was lifted.

Hallucinogenic Accounting

Company acquisitions of additional licensed producers became especially important, because International Financial Reporting Standards (IFRS) include the "Fair Value Gain from Growth of Biological Assets" as a revenue item in determining gross profit. Thus, the more a Canadian cannabis company grows the more gross revenue it will report on its income statement.

Under IFRS biological assets consist of actively growing cannabis plants to be harvested as agricultural produce. The average grow cycle of plants up to the point of harvest is approximately twelve weeks. Plants in production are valued at fair value less cost to complete and cost to sell, where fair value represents the Company's selling price per gram of dried cannabis. The percentage of the growing cycle completed is used to determine the percentages (therefore dollar amounts) of costs and revenue to recognize on a cannabis company income statement and balance sheet.

All Canadian cannabis companies initially used IFRS instead of GAAP. They therefore enjoyed a liberal recognition of revenue and were also allowed to capitalize some expenses instead of recognizing them in their income statements. An accounting system that artificially inflates revenue and lowers expenses is a dream come true for those wanting to pitch a company's stock.

Al Rosen, PhD, a well-known and highly respected Canadian author, forensic accountant and York University professor, has referred to Canadian cannabis companies' use of IFRS as "hallucinogenic accounting." His books $WINDLERS$ and EASY PREY INVESTORS note in great detail past schemes that have cost investors massive amounts of money and should be required reading for all investors. Rosen believes that many of the people who promoted Canadian scams in the past became involved in the cannabis sector.

Five Companies Dominate Canada

Five Canadian companies quickly established dominance over that country's cannabis industry. Those companies were Aphria (APHA), Aurora Cannabis (ACB), Canopy Growth (CGC), Cronos (CRON), and Tilray (TLRY). They captured investment dollars at a pace seldom seen in any country in history as they became the face of the cannabis industry.

Canopy Growth Corporation

The Canadian cannabis company with the largest market capitalization is Canopy Growth Corporation (CGC). The company was originally founded by Bruce Linton and Chuck Rifici in April 2014 as Tweed Marijuana Inc. It became the first of Canada's cannabis companies to be publicly traded when it listed 4,687,500 shares on the TSX Venture Exchange. GMP Securities, L.P. was the lead underwriter and brought it public at C$3.20 per share raising C$15 million.

It was one of the first 13 companies listed with Health Canada as a Licensed Producer (LP) under the Marijuana for Medical Purposes Regulations. Its sole cultivation facility was in Smith Falls, Ontario at an old Hershey plant.

Linton was chairman of the board and Rifici was president and CEO of Tweed at the time it was listed. Linton owned 10.27% or 3,621,712 shares and Rifici owned 22.09% or 7,789,610 shares. Rifici had served as a CFO for several companies prior to Tweed and was expected to run the business, while Linton was expected to provide oversight. Before the end of 2014, however, Rifici was gone from the company and replaced by Linton. Interestingly, neither of the founders had any apparent employment history in agriculture or marketing.

Rifici is rumored to have sold all his shares in the company shortly after his departure. He went on to be involved in a number of other companies in the Canadian cannabis sector, but his stature in the industry diminished with time. Meanwhile, Linton as CEO of the cannabis company with the largest market capitalization became the leading spokesperson for the sector and frequent guest on CNBC until his ouster from Canopy in the summer of 2019.

At the end of its first fiscal year on March 31, 2015, Tweed had C$47.7 million in total assets, nothing in goodwill, C$41.4 million in equity, C$2.4 million in revenue, a loss of C$0.29 per share, an operating loss of C$8.2 million and negative operating free cash flow of C$10.9 million. Despite these less than awesome financials, Canopy was able to attract investors anxious to be put money into the cannabis sector, because they alone were publicly traded on a Canadian stock exchange and on the U.S. over-the-counter (OTC) market. On May 24, 2018 Canopy uplisted and became the first Canadian cannabis corporation to trade on the New York Stock Exchange (NYSE).

On August 28, 2015 Tweed completed the first of many acquisitions when it acquired Bedrocan of Canada. A few weeks later Tweed officially changed its company name to Canopy Growth Corporation and embarked on an expansion program that would do justice to its name.

On October 1, 2015 it acquired MedCann Access and from that point until 2021 it went on a shopping spree for domestic and foreign cannabis companies. During that 6-year span it seemed that at least once a week Canopy issued a press release or held a press conference to announce another acquisition or joint venture somewhere in the world where great opportunities awaited them and their shareholders.

Canopy's early emphasis on extensive investor relations, news releases and use of the media became the template for all cannabis companies to follow. Canopy issued only 24 news releases in 2017; but, in 2018 it took investor relations to a level probably not seen since the days of P. T. Barnum, when it issued 108. It issued news releases announcing just about everything except what CEO Linton had for breakfast on Canada Day in 2018. Canopy continued churning out press releases at a rapid pace issuing 83 in 2019, 60 in 2020, and 24 in the first six months of 2021. If cannabis stocks traded on the basis of the number of news releases issued by a company, Canopy would trade at the richest valuation!

On a conference call accompanying a Canopy earnings release in August 2017, CEO Linton and his CFO were asked when they expected the company to earn a profit and generate positive operating free cash flow. After a notable period of silence, Linton commented that their primary concern was growing enough cannabis to meet the coming demand for marijuana, which was expected to far exceed supply. He then made a statement that Canopy was following in Amazon's footsteps by focusing on growth and not thinking about profits and cash flow.

Linton's comparison of Canopy Growth to Amazon is a view that is shared by a vast majority of cannabis company CEOs, investment bankers, and owners of cannabis stocks. They firmly believe their performance cannot be measured using conventional yardsticks, because they are in the early stage of an explosive growth cycle guaranteed to yield huge profits.

Constellation Brands

From its inception through the summer of 2017 Canopy incurred substantial losses on its income statement accompanied by negative cash flow from operations. It was able to fund itself during this period by issuing stock and debt. On November 2, 2017 Constellation Brands (STZ) acquired an equity interest in CGC sufficient enough to allow Canopy to continue its cash burn.

Initially, Constellation invested $191.3 million in 18,876,901 shares of Canopy on November 2, 2017 at a price of $12.9783 per share. As a part of that investment STZ was also granted warrants with 30-month expirations that allowed it to buy an additional 9,438,450 shares at the same per share price on August 1, 2018 and another 9,438,450 shares on February 1, 2019. On June 20, 2018 SYZ then bought $200 million in 4.25% senior notes due 2023 convertible into Canopy common shares at the rate of 23.742 common shares per $1,000 of face value.

The abovementioned Constellation investments helped alleviate Canopy's immediate cash flow needs; however, a November 2, 2018 purchase of 104,500,000 CGC shares for $4 billion cured Canopy's cash flow problem for the foreseeable future. Constellation investments in Canopy gave a clear vote of confidence to Canopy management's plan to become the dominant cannabis company in the world. Tapping into Constellation Brands' treasury was like hitting the Powerball Lottery for Bruce Linton and he wasted very little time before deciding to spend some of that money on his growth fixation.

On April 18, 2019 Linton announced Canopy had reached a complex arrangement agreement to eventually acquire 100% of Acreage Holdings, which he said was the leading U.S. multi-state-operator (MSO). The first step in that process payment of $300 million or $2.55 per share to Acreage shareholders for the right to acquire their shares at an exchange ratio of 0.5818 shares of Canopy per share of Acreage. At prices prevailing at that time, that gave the transaction a value of $3.4 billion.

Closing of the transaction would depend on a Laws changing (Triggering Event) to permit the transaction. The arrangement agreement was approved by Acreage and Canopy shareholders on June 20, 2019.

This unique "Triggering Event" deal was ballyhooed as the first in a likely series of deals by Canadian firms. It was especially noteworthy and ascribed as a harbinger because of the Acreage's politically savvy board of directors. Acreage directors included former speaker of the U.S. House of Representatives, John Boehner; former Massachusetts Governor, Bill Weld; and former Canadian Prime Minister, Brian Mulroney. At the time of the Acreage IPO, Boehner and Weld each owned or controlled 625,000 shares worth $15.625 million at the IPO offering price of $25, while Mulroney owned or controlled 280,000 shares worth $7.0 million. Interestingly, Mulroney and Boehner generally opposed marijuana legalization during their political careers; however, they converted to seeing the medical benefits of marijuana. Some believe Mulroney and Boehner changing their tune was a sign of progress, while others saw it as more fuel for their cynical views of politics.

The performances of Acreage and Canopy deteriorated markedly soon after shareholders approved the arrangement agreement. Acreage, in particular, encountered significant cash flow problems that forced them to curtail any expansion. Acreage was managed by Wall Streeters who proved to be inept at cultivating cannabis as evidenced by Florida operations.

On January 4, 2019 Acreage Holdings acquired Nature's Way Nursery of Miami, Florida for $67 million. Acreage paid $63 million in cash and $4 million in High Street Capital Partners Units. Nature's Way was a Florida licensed seed-to-sale company without a single dispensary.

Acreage proved it was unable to cultivate and produce cannabis products as demonstrated by the fact it only had one dispensary in the state two years after its Florida acquisition and its total cannabis sales for the week ending January 7, 2021 were 222 ounces of flower! It is not surprising that on February 25, 2021 Acreage announced it had signed a definitive agreement with Red White & Bloom Brands (RWB) to sell its Florida operations. The deal calls for RWB is making an upfront cash payment of $5 million, plus an additional $20 million in cash, $7 million in stock and $28 million in promissory notes. Observers were quick to point out that Acreage's failure to succeed in a limited licenses state like Florida was a very bad omen.

It is not surprising that Linton was fired by Canopy's board on July 3, 2019. The $300 million upfront payment he engineered for Acreage shareholders was an absolute gift and Acreage was a horrible acquisition choice. The original arrangement agreement has been heavily amended, but is not worth detailing here.

STZ investors questioned the wisdom of making such a huge commitment to the unproven cannabis sector, especially since it had to borrow the $4 billion to make the late 2018 investment. STZ shareholders voted with their feet by selling shares. STZ shares traded at $200.58 on the day the Canopy investment was announced, but by January 18, 2019 STZ had fallen 18% to $164.15.

Constellation Brands shareholders had been well served by the Sands' Brothers leadership and their apparent Midas touch, but they questioned the wisdom of taking such a big stake in an unproven company like Canopy. STZ shareholders' reservations turned out to be correct, as much of the $4+ billion invested was washed down the drain in following years.

Canopy Financials

Since its inception, Canopy has been led by people with a dream, but no meaningful business management expertise. This lack of experience running a business is evident in a balance sheet and income statement that reflect poor operating results.

Canopy management proved adept at buying companies with other people's money, but then again anyone can do that. CGC management did not demonstrate their purchases were good deals for CGC shareholders. The financial results confirm that management was only interested in growth.

Total assets grew from C$47.7 million at the end of its 2015 fiscal year to C$6.8 billion as of March 31, 2020. In that 63-month period CGC added C$1.9 billion in goodwill, which can be thought of as a premium CGC paid to acquire other companies. As should be expected, the growth in Canopy's balance sheet was accompanied by growth in revenue. In fact, revenue rose from C$2.4 million in fiscal 2015 to an annualized rate of C$546.7 million in its fiscal 2021, which ended March 31, 2021.

The net result of CGC management focusing on growth was that income and cash flow suffered. CGC had an operating loss in each of its first six years in business and the size of the loss grew from C$8.2 million in 2015 to C$1.2 billion in fiscal 2021. In fiscal 2019 it's reported a C$0.6 billion operating loss and in 2020 it lost C$1.7 billion. Canopy's horrible operating results are also illustrated by negative operating free cash flow soaring from C$10.9 million in fiscal 2015 to C$535 in 2019, C$773 million in 2020, and C$466 million in 2021.

The horrible financial performance of Canopy, the oldest vertically integrated cannabis company with the largest market capitalization, casts a cloud of uncertainty over the economic prospects of the entire Canadian cannabis industry. Dreams of incredible riches from cannabis in Canada are being seriously questioned by investors. The all-time high and low closing prices of Canopy Growth have been $56.89 on October 15, 2018 and $1.15 on September 2, 2015.

Since its inception, Canopy has consistently lost money and burned cash. As of March 31, 2021 it had an accumulated deficit of C$6.1 billion. If a company with an early mover advantage, a virtually unlimited amount of equity capital, and the management expertise of experienced S&P 500 company executives from Constellation Brands cannot earn a profit, can any company succeed?

Tilray

Tilray (TLRY) was also one the 13 original companies to be approved by Health Canada as a Licensed Producer (LP) under the Marijuana for Medical Purposes Regulations in 2014. Tilray's operations are located in the Vancouver Island town of Nanaimo, Canada; however, it's registered and records office is located in Seattle, Washington.

Tilray's roots trace back to the founding of Privateer Holdings in 2010 in Seattle as a private equity firm focused exclusively on building a portfolio of global brands in the cannabis space. The three people who started Privateer, Brendan Kennedy, Michael Bluh and Christian Groh, had backgrounds in finance and high tech and no experience in agriculture or cannabis.

In 2011 Privateer was able to scrape together enough money to acquire Leafly, a cannabis website designed to educate consumers and help them locate cannabis products. At the time of its acquisition Leafly's website had about 100,000 visits per month.

In December 2013 Privateer completed its first round of funding, $7 million in Series A, which enabled it to form Tilray of Canada in April 2014 and enter into 30-year licensing deal with the estate of Bob Marley for Marley Natural products. In April 2015, Privateer raised $75 million in a Series B and among the investors was Founders Fund headed by Peter Thiel. In October 2016 Privateer raised $46 million via a convertible debt offering. In January 2018 it closed a $100 Series C funding round and at the same time incorporated Tilray in Delaware as a subsidiary of Privateer Holdings.

Privateer thus raised a total of $226 million from private equity investors by January 2018. Its own cash flow up to early 2018 was entirely dependent on raising additional private equity funds, selling assets, and/or receiving cash dividends and management fees from Tilray. It alone did not have the cash resources or borrowing capacity necessary to inject money into Tilray like Constellation Brands did with Canopy.

Tilray IPO

On July 19, 2018 Tilray went public in an IPO on the Canadian Securities Exchange (CSE) and simultaneously on NASDAQ, where it became the first marijuana related company to IPO in the United States. Tilray offered 9,000,000 Subordinated Voting Shares (SUB) in its IPO. The offering in Canada was led by BMO Nesbitt Burns Inc. and Eight Capital; while the U.S. Offering was conducted by Cowen and Company LLC, Roth Capital Partners LLC and Northland Securities, Inc.

Following the offering there were 91,794,042 shares outstanding composed of 16,666,667 Multiple Voting Shares, MVS, entitled to 10 votes per share but convertible into only 1 SUB share; and, 75,127,375 SUB shares. Privateer owned all the MVS shares and 58,333,333 SUB shares following the offering, representing 81.7% of all the shares outstanding. The 9,000,000 shares issued meant that the float or tradable shares amounted to only 9.8% of the total shares outstanding. The IPO did include a 180-day lock-up of shares owned by officers and directors. Tilray went public at $17 per share and popped to a high of $31.80 on its first day of trading.

Tilray first captured investors' attention on September 18, 2018 when the U.S. Drug Enforcement Administration, DEA, approved its importation of marijuana from Canada for medical research at the University of California San Diego Center for Medicinal Cannabis Research to study the safety, tolerability and efficacy of marijuana for treatment of essential tremor. Essential Tremor (ET) is a neurological movement disorder characterized by involuntary and rhythmic shaking. In making the announcement Tilray noted that ET affects about 1.3 million people in the U.S.

Tilray chose this occasion to mention that studies using Tilray cannabis were taking place at the University of British Columbia Okanagan on the impact of cannabis on post-traumatic stress disorder, while others were being conducted at the University of Sydney in Australia on chemotherapy nausea reduction and at The Hospital for Sick Children in Toronto on pediatric epilepsy. Amazingly, this news caught the imagination of investors and caused shares of TLRY to explode higher.

On September 18, 2018 TLRY closed at $154.98 on volume of 20 million shares. The next day TLRY traded from $151.40 to $300.00 on volume of 32 million shares and trading in it was halted five times. It closed at $214.06 up $59.08 or 38.1% on the day. The September 19, 2018 intraday high of $300 gave Tilray an absurd market capitalization of $37.5 billion, which dwarfed any of its Canadian peers.

By the end of the year Tilray was trading around $80. This was well below the mid-September levels, but still up about fivefold from the July IPO. It that six-month period a number of people in Seattle became so-called "Tilionaires."

There was growing concern that Tilray shares would experience significant downward pressure when the looming 180-day lock-up expired to allay fears of a surge in share sales, on January 14, 2019, just days prior to the lock-up expiration, Privateer announced it would not be selling any of its 75 million shares when the lock-up expired.

It said it believed in Tilray's long-term global growth strategy and pioneering role in shaping the future of the legal cannabis industry, and had no plans to register, sell or distribute its Tilray shares during the first half of 2019.

Tilray also said that when they decide to distribute shares they we will do so in an orderly and deliberate manner to maximize tax-efficiency considerations for Privateer investors, while also taking into consideration potential impacts on Tilray's public float. That statement would be repeated by many other cannabis company CEOs in following months as their own lockups neared expiration.

This news initially sent TLRY shares up, but then market participants realized there were still about 7.9 million non-Privateer shares that could be sold. On January 15, 2019, the day the original lock-up expired, TLRY shares closed down $17.27 or 17.3%. In the 30 days prior to its lock-up expiration the average daily trading volume of TLRY was 2.5 million shares, but on the day the lock-up expired volume was 15.2 million or 6x normal volume.

The wild swings in TLRY stock serve as a reminder of what can happen to share prices when only a small fraction of a company's shares trade. Additionally, the price action at time of lock-up expiration shows what can happen when lock-up shares represent a significant percentage of the float/tradable shares and holders of those shares decide to sell.

Tilray Deals

On Dec. 18, 2018, Tilray signed a partnership with Swiss drug maker Novartis AG (NVS) to research, develop, and distribute medical marijuana around the world. The two companies announced they were teaming up to commercialize Tilray's non-smokable medical marijuana products, develop new products under a partnership brand, and spread awareness about cannabis to pharmacists and physicians. News of this deal sent Tilray's share price soaring by as much as 12 percent

Two days later on December 20, Tilray announced it was teaming up with the world's largest brewer, Anheuser-Busch InBev (BUD), to develop cannabis-infused non-alcoholic drinks for the Canadian market. As part of the deal, each company invested $50 million in research. At the time of the Anheuser-Busch InBev announcement, market analysts were estimating that the cannabis-infused beverage industry could see annual U.S. sales of $500 million in the next five years. Shares of Tilray climbed 15.32% following this news.

The deals between Tilray, Novartis AG and Anheuser-Busch InBev came after a much-anticipated decision by Canada to legalize recreational marijuana edibles, beverages and smoking products. The fact that Tilray was selected by BUD and NVS greatly enhanced TLRY credibility even though the commitments were miniscule compared to Constellation Brands commitment with Canopy.

Tilray was one of the best performing IPOs in 2018. It came public at $17 and it closed that year at $70.54, so it more than quadrupled in less than six months. Its stock performance deteriorated significantly following its initial flurry and reached an all-time low of $2.47 at the close on March 18, 2020.

Tilray Financials

For its 2015, 2016, 2017, and 2018 fiscal years Tilray reported total revenue of C$5.4 million, C$12.6 million, C$20.5 million, and C$41.9 million, respectively. It experienced significant revenue growth in 2019 as it reached C$167.0 million, and in 2020 it had C$210.5 million in revenue.

Tilray reported net operating losses for each of its first three years. It lost C$14.9 million in 2015, C$7.9 million in 2016, and C$7.8 million in 2017. Given these losses it is not shocking that Brendan Kennedy, the Executive Chairman of Privateer and CEO of Tilray, said he was overwhelmed by the positive reception Tilray received in its IPO.

Tilray's early losses were a harbinger of more to come. It had a loss of C$67.7 in 2018, C$321.2 million in 2019, and C$271.1 million in 2020.

The losses during its first six years of existence gave rise to an accumulated deficit of C$730.1. Shareholders' equity plummeted to only C$373.9 million at the end of 2020.

Amazingly, the S-1 Registration Statement Tilray filed with the SEC as a part of its IPO showed that it had negative net worth at the end of its 2017 fiscal year, which was its third complete year in business. Its December 31, 2017 statement showed C$31.6 million in paid in capital, C$3.8 million in accumulated other comprehensive income and an accumulated deficit of C$40.5. Those equity accounts netted to a negative C$4.9 million! It is doubtful the students of Benjamin Graham would invest in such a company.

The fact that Privateer Holdings allowed the equity account of Tilray to go negative on the last day of its 2017 fiscal year should have alerted investors. It conveyed a distinct impression that Privateer was not willing or able to fund its dream of making Tilray the leading worldwide brand. Without Privateer, Tilray had to rely on issuing more debt and/or equity to fund continued operating losses and negative operating free cash flows.

Besides losing most of its equity capital, Tilray also consistently bled cash. It generated negative operating cash flows of C$7.7 million in 2015, C$3.3 million in 2016, C$6.0 in 2017, C$46.3 in 2018, C$258.1 in 2019, and C$129.4 in 2020. Its cumulative negative cash flow from operations for the six years ending 2020 therefore amount to C$450.8 million.

Tilray was totally dependant on Privateer Holdings as a source of funds from its inception until its IPO. In turn, Privateer was totally reliant on raising cash from private equity investors to funnel into Tilray, which then burned through that cash.

Privateer Holdings and its investors became awash in paper wealth, but cash poor. In fact, Privateer's marshalling its precious cash is probably why Tilray's equity account was allowed to go negative at the end of 2017.

Frankly, the IPO looks as if it saved Tilray from folding up its tent and taking its shareholders and Privateer down with it in 2018. Thanks to that IPO a cash flow crisis was averted in 2018 and allowed Privateer to announce that it would not sell any of its 75 million unlocked shares during the first six months of 2019. Furthermore, the IPO gave investors faith in Tilray and allowed it to tap the debt and equity markets to cover its continuing cash drain.

Tilray's financials raise a number of serious questions. First, how could the SEC allow a four-year old company to register and go public with a negative equity account? Second, how could Nasdaq allow such a company to list on its stock exchange? Third, why did Privateer Holdings allow Tilray to show negative equity? Fourth, could Tilray ever earn a profit and generate a positive operating free cash flow? Fifth, do investors really believe that Tilray is about to discover miracle cures for diseases that have escaped discovery by GW Pharma, which has been doing pure research on cannabis for 20+ years and only just recently made a breakthrough discovery? Sixth, why did Novartis and Anheuser-Busch

InBev decide to partner with Privateer?

Aphria

Given Tilray's terrible financial results it is not surprising that its leaders decided to merge with Aphria. On December 16, 2020, before the markets opened, Tilray announced it entered into a definitive agreement to merge with Aphria, Inc.

The merger was structured as a reverse acquisition of Tilray since Aphria shareholders would receive 0.8381 shares of Tilray for every share of Aphria they own. The agreement terms gave Tilray shareholders a 23% premium based on closing prices of each company's shares the day before the announcement. On December 15 Tilray closed at $7.87, while Aphria closed at $8.12. On the day of the announcement Tilray rose to $9.33, while Aphria fell to $8.05.

Unlike Canopy and Tilray, Aphria was actually started by experienced farmers who made their living growing other things before cannabis became legal. Aphria Inc. was incorporated under the Business Corporations Act (Alberta) on June 22, 2011 as Black Sparrow Capital Corp. (Black Sparrow) and was continued in Ontario on December 1, 2014. On December 2, 2014, via a reverse takeover (RTO) Aphria became an operating company. Just days prior to that RTO, Aphria was awarded its license from Health Canada to cultivate, process and sell medical marijuana under the provisions of the Marihuana for Medical Purposes Regulations (MMPR).

Aphria's headquarters are in Leamington, Ontario, which is where its primary cultivation facilities are also located. Aphria is one of the original Canadian licensed producers and among the first to offer cannabis products. It is focused on producing and selling medical marijuana through a two-pronged growth strategy that includes both retail sales and wholesale channels. Retail sales are conducted through Aphria's online store as well as telephone orders. Wholesale shipments are sold to other MMPR licensed producers.

Aphria's leaders recognized that the Canadian market was not sizeable enough to support all LPs; therefore, it was among the first to decide to expand internationally. It recognized the immense potential in the United States particularly Florida and it took quick action.

On November 8, 2016 over 70% of Florida voters approved a constitutional amendment legalizing the use of medical marijuana. On June 23, 2017 Florida's Governor signed into law Senate Bill 8-A, a 48 page statute know as the Medical Marijuana Implementing bill.

While Florida was codifying the intent of its voters, Aphria on April 5, 2017 announced a $25 million investment in DFMMJ Investments, Ltd. (DFMMJ). The latter then acquired all or substantially all of the assets of Chestnut Hill Tree Farm LLC, through its subsidiary DFMMJ Investments, LLC. The $25 million was combined with an additional $35 million raised in a brokered private placement led by Clarus Securities Inc. and used to launch Aphria's expansion strategy into the United States cannabis market via an entity to be renamed Liberty Health Sciences Inc. (Liberty), which was designed to operate in the United States under the brand Aphria USA.

The business combination was completed on July 20, 2017, when 1006397 B.C. Ltd. (Subco), a British Columbia company and wholly-owned subsidiary of SecureCom, completed a business combination with DFMMJ Investments, Ltd. (Holdco) whereby SecureCom acquired all of the issued and outstanding shares of Holdco by way of a three-cornered amalgamation. Holdco amalgamated with Subco under the British Columbia Business Corporation Act (BCBCA) to form a wholly-owned subsidiary of SecureCom named Liberty Health Sciences USA Ltd. Concurrent with the Business Combination, SecureCom changed its name to Liberty Health Sciences Inc. and DFMMJ Investments, LLC (d/b/a Liberty Health Sciences Florida, LTD.) became a wholly-owned subsidiary. Liberty Health Science common shares began trading on the Canadian Securities Exchange under the symbol LHS on July 26, 2017 at $0.48.

Within months of Aphria investing in a publicly held Florida medical marijuana company, legal problems began to surface. In particular, Canadian nationals who were officers and directors of Liberty Health Sciences experienced trouble entering the United States because of marijuana being labeled a Schedule 1 substance. These difficulties at the border encouraged Aphria to dispose of its ownership position. Their sale was also precipitated by the fact that Aphria wanted to uplist to the New York Stock Exchange (NYSE), and the NYSE would not list any company with a direct ownership interest in the production, processing or distribution of marijuana in the US. Furthermore, the Toronto Stock Exchange (TSX) required Aphria to divest its U.S ownership interests to maintain its listing on that exchange. All ownership ties between Aphria and Liberty Health Sciences ended in February 2019.

As Aphria was exiting Florida it was actively engaged in acquiring ownership interests in Latin America and the Caribbean. It made numerous investments in Argentina, Brazil, Colombia and Jamaica that became known as their LATAM Holdings. These acquisitions became the subject of a scathing report by researchers who claimed these transactions were skimming operations by Aphria insiders and friends of those insiders.

A widely distributed report by Hindenburg Research and Quintessential Capital Management alleged that Aphria management participated in a shell game controlled by insiders raiding company coffers to line their own pockets. The report titled "Aphria: A Shell Game with a Cannabis Business on the Side" was published on December 3, 2018.

Aphria denied the allegations and claimed they were a ploy by malicious short sellers to knock down the price of Aphria shares. Aphria traded 1.7 million shares the day before the report was released and closed at $7.90. On the day the report was released 35.5 million shares traded and the stock closed down 23.4% at $6.05. The next day it closed at $4.51. On December 6 it traded as low as $3.75. It took until January 31, 2019 for APHA stock to close above its December 2, 2018 price.

In mid-February 2019 a special committee appointed to review the LATAM allegations concluded the purchase prices were on the higher end of an acceptable range compared to similar acquisitions and indicated the carrying value of those acquired assets needed to be assessed going forward. In the wake of this investigation Aphria's CEO and two of its co-founders left APHA.

In April 2019 Aphria took an impairment charge of $50 million directly related to its LATAM assets. In announcing the charge Aphia said it arose from the company's reassessment of the discount rate and financial forecasts for the LATAM entities due to new financial information received by the special committee who reviewed the LATAM transaction.

The impairment charge and management shakeup precipitated a deep and prolonged selloff of Aphria shares. The closing price of Aphria shares just prior to the announcement was $10.10. The share price fell to a low of $2.13 on March 18, 2020, almost a full year later. The share price did not get back to its pre-impairment level until January 14, 2021, 21 months later, when it closed at $12.11.

Aphria Financials

Aphria experienced steady growth in revenue from 2015 through 2018. Revenue rose from C$0.6 million in its 2015 fiscal year to C$8.4 million in 2016 then to C$20.4 million in 2017 and C$36.9 million in 2018. With Canada's full legalization on October 17, 2018 Aphria revenue accelerated dramatically to C$237.1 million in 2019 and C$543.3 million in 2020. Based on its first nine months of fiscal 2021, Aphria was expected to achieve revenue of C$613.2 for its fiscal year ended May 31, 2021.

Unfortunately, the growth in Aphria revenue was more than offset by expenses. Aphria operating losses amounted to C$3.4 million in 2015, C$1.1 million in 2016, C$1.4 million in 2017, C$12.2 million in 2018, C$145.2 million in 2019, and C$66.1 million in 2020. In the nine-month ended February 28, 2021 it recorded an operating loss of C$90.8 million. The operating losses combined with impairment charges such that on February 28, 2021 Aphria's balance sheet showed it had incurred accumulated losses of C$601.2 million since its inception.

Besides consistently losing money, Aphria also proved adept at burning cash. Its cash provided from operations was a negative C$5.4 million in 2015 and C$1.0 in 2016. In 2017 it managed to have positive cash provided from operations; however, it amounted to only C$5.3 and it was offset by the negative C$5.6 million reported in the following year. Negative cash flow from operations accelerated in 2019 as Aphria reported a drain of C$55.1 million, which was followed by an even greater drain of C$133.8 million in 2020. Through its first nine months of fiscal 2021 it showed negative cash flow from operations of C$64.8 million. The cumulative negative cash provided from Aphria operations for the 6 ¾ years of its existence was therefore C$260.4 million.

Tilray Aphria Merger

Unlike Canopy Growth, neither Tilray nor Aphria attracted a "Daddy Warbucks" like Constellation brands. Furthermore, both were finding it more difficult to raise money externally to fund their cash burns. It was not surprising that they decided to join forces and merge the fact that the newly merged company was named Tilray is effectively an admission that the Aphria name had been badly tarnished by the events surrounding the LATAM transactions.

In recent years both companies had focused their attention outside Canada. They realized the size of the Canadian market was simply too small, so they increasingly expended time and resources on establishing a global presence. At the time of the merger Tilray stated it had cultivation facilities in Portugal and selling agreements with established pharmaceutical distributors in Argentina, Australia, Brazil, Canada, Chile, Croatia, Cyprus, Czech Republic, Denmark, Germany, Israel, New Zealand, Peru, Poland, Portugal, Spain, Africa, Switzerland, United States, Malta, and United Kingdom. They intend to leverage those existing operations while establishing new ones.

In December 2020, just a few months prior to the closing the Tilray merger, Aphria showed it remained focused on the United States marketplace when it acquired SweetWater Brewing Company for $250 million in cash and $50 million in Aphria stock. SweetWater is one of the largest craft brewers in the U.S. based on volume and headquartered in Atlanta, Georgia.

On April 30, 2021 the Aphria/Tilray merger was consummated. For their most recent 12 months they had combined revenues of $685 million (C$874 million). Tilray believes it can dominate the global markets by leveraging their existing international operations.

Aurora Cannabis Inc.

A fourth significant publicly held Canadian cannabis company is Aurora Cannabis Inc. It was originally incorporated under the Business Corporations Act of British Columbia on December 21, 2006 using the name Milk Capital Corp. On September 3, 2010 Milk Capital changed its name to Prescient Mining Corp. Aurora Cannabis Inc. officially came into being via a RTO on December 9, 2014 when Aurora Marijuana Inc. shares were exchanged for Prescient shares and the later changed its name to Aurora Cannabis, Inc.

In the year preceding their exchange of shares both Prescient and Aurora Marijuana were losing money and dissipating cash. Aurora Marijuana showed no income and a loss of C$1,823,535 for the period from September 11, 2013 (its date of incorporation) until June 30, 2014 and an additional loss of C$925,157 for the three months ended September 30, 2014. For the same time periods its operating free cash flows were a negative C$965,106 and a negative C$823,319. On September 30, 2014 Aurora Marijuana only had C$79,801 in cash and showed accumulated losses of C$2,748,106 on its balance sheet.

Prescient Mining Corp. was certainly not doing well financially prior to the share exchange. In the three months ended September 30, 2014 it had no revenue, an operating loss of C$542,732 and negative operating free cash flow of C$276,968. Its balance sheet showed it had accumulated losses of C$2,042,236. Prescient did, however, have C$1,622,430 in cash and cash equivalents.

Immediately following the RTO, Aurora Cannabis embarked on a campaign to raise capital to fund construction of a 54,000 square foot indoor growing, production and distribution facility in Cremona (population 457). Aurora became the first cannabis producer in its province to obtain a Health Canada license. Its original Production License from Health Canada limited Aurora production to 5,500 kilograms of marijuana per year.

For the first few years of its existence Aurora seemed to tread water as it focused on production at its Cremona facility and raising funds. It is interesting that Chuck Rifici, the co-founder of Canopy Growth, joined the board of Aurora in September 2015 shortly after his departure from Canopy. His appointment suggests Aurora might have wanted to take a look at Canopy's playbook to help it develop a game plan. While Rifici stayed on Aurora's board for only the 2016 fiscal year, it was long enough to create a lasting rivalry between Aurora and Canopy. In fact, a number of people in Canadian cannabis sector consider Aurora the western version of Canopy.

Aurora Financials

Aurora had no revenue in its 2015 fiscal year ended June 30, 2015 and only C$1.4 million in 2016. Its operating losses were C$5.4 million in 2015 and C$4.6 million in 2016; and, cash flow provided from operations amounted to a negative C$3.3 and C$6.8 million in the respective years. These less than impressive financial results did not prevent Aurora from raising funds.

Aurora's financing ability got off to a rough start when it retracted an April 2, 2015 press release that it had secured a C$3.5 million bridge loan from Century Services, Inc. Somehow, that loan fell through and on April 10th Aurora issued a press release which stated that its April 2 announcement was issued prematurely. It subsequently secured C$1 million in bridge financing from other parties. A second financing took place on June 16, 2015 when it raised $2 million in unsecured debt from its CEO Terry Booth and companies controlled by Booth and Steve Dobler, who was president of Aurora. A third financing was completed at the end of 2015 via a nonbrokered private placement for C$4.8 million. The Aurora fund raising machine really kicked into high gear with five completed transactions in calendar 2016. The money from these financings was used to fund acquisitions, joint ventures and replace cash evaporating from negative operating cash flow.

In fiscal 2017 Aurora decided to implement a strategy focused on growth. Its goal was to become a leader in the Canadian and international cannabis space via vertical and horizontal integration. Aurora implemented that strategy through a steady stream of acquisitions such that it now has operations in more than 20 countries.

The results of Aurora implementing its global growth strategy are evidenced by its financial statements. Total assets grew from C$18.4 million in fiscal 2016 to $322.7 million in 2017 before soaring to C$1.9 billion in 2018, and C$5.5 billion in 2019.

The rapid growth in assets occurred through acquisitions of companies well above book value. As a result, intangible assets and goodwill exploded on Aurora's balance sheet. Its fiscal year end statement for 2017 showed only C$31.1 million in intangible assets, but at the end of 2019 they amounted to C$688.4 million. During the same span, goodwill grew from C$41.1 million to C$3.2 billion!

Aurora relied entirely on external funding to accomplish its acquisitions. In the above two years ending June 30, 2019 it added C$200+ million in convertible debt and C$120+ million in loans. It also increased the number of shares outstanding by 177.5% or 650.9 million. By the end of its 2019 fiscal year it had more than one billion shares outstanding.

In March 2019 Aurora obtained the services of Nelson Pelz, a billionaire known for expertise in the consumer goods sector. Aurora awarded him options in return for his assistance in pursuing strategic partnerships. To the dismay of ACB shareholders the ACB association with Pelz bore no identifiable fruit and ended in 2020.

On May 11, 2020 Aurora completed a one-for-twelve (1:12) reverse share split of all of its issued and outstanding common shares, resulting in a reduction in the issued and outstanding shares from 1,321,072,394 to 110,089,377. Without this reverse stock split Aurora's stock could have been delisted on the NYSE, since it was trading below $1.

Fiscal 2020 was a disaster for Aurora. It had revenue of C$323.2 million which was up 19.2% from its fiscal 2019; but, despite that revenue, it had an operating loss of C$491.0 million. Its cash provided from operations was also negative at C$338.0 million.

The real disaster in 2020, however, was the huge write-off taken by Aurora. It recognized impairment charges of C$2.8 billion and reported an after-tax loss of $3.3 billion for its fiscal 2020. Impairment of intangible assets amounted to C$276 and goodwill write-offs totaled C$2.244 billion. The after-tax loss for 2020 meant that during the first six years of its existence Aurora accumulated losses of C$3.6 billion.

Things did not improve for Aurora in the immediate aftermath of it fiscal 2020 calamity. In fact, in the first nine months of its fiscal 2021 it reported an operating loss of C$232.3 million and negative cash provided from operations of C$230 million.

Aurora Cannabis moved its listing from the NYSE to the NASDAQ on May 25, 2021 while retaining its ACB trading symbol. It stated the move was a part of its cost efficiency initiative and aligned the company with other cannabis peers on an exchange noted for innovative, growth-oriented companies. Since inception, ACB shares have traded as low as $0.03 and as high as $18.98. Its average daily trading volume is now about 7 million shares per day.

Cronos

Cronos Group Inc. was incorporated in the Province of British Columbia in 2012 and under the British Columbia Business Corporations Act with principal executive offices at 111 Peter St. Street, Suite 300, Toronto, Ontario, M5V 2H1. The Company's common shares are listed on the Toronto Stock Exchange (TSX) and Nasdaq Global Market (NASDAQ) under the ticker symbol CRON.

Cronos is a Canadian Licensed Producer (LP) and cultivates, processes, and markets cannabis and cannabis-derived products for the medical and adult-use markets primarily in Canada. It also manufactures and markets hemp-derived supplements and cosmetic products through e-commerce, retail, and hospitality partner channels in the US under its Lord Jones, Happy Dance and Peace brands. The company's marijuana offerings include dried cannabis, pre-rolls, and cannabis extracts through wholesale and direct-to-client channels under its wellness platform, PEACE NATURALS; and operates under two adult-use brands, COVE and Spinach. The company also exports dried cannabis and cannabis oils to Germany, Israel, and Australia.

In December 2018 Altria (MO) bought a 45% ownership position in Cronos for $1.8 billion. Altria also acquired a warrant allowing it to increase its position to about 55% at a price of $19 per share.

Altria manufactures and sells cigarettes, oral tobacco products, and wine in the United States. Its brands include Marlboro, Black & Mild, Copenhagen, Skoal, Red Seal, and Husky. The company also produces and sells under the Chateau Ste. Michelle and 14 Hands wines. It imports and markets Antinori, Torres, and Villa Maria Estate wines, as well as Nicolas Feuillatte Champagne in the United States.

If Constellation Brands (STZ) is Canopy Growth's "Daddy Warbucks" then Altria is Cronos "Daddy Warbucks on Steroids." Altria annual revenue of $89 billion and after-tax income of $4.4 billion are twice as large as those of Constellation.

Cronos Financials

Unlike the other large Canadian LPs, Cronos actually showed accumulated profits from its inception thru 2020. During those years it earned C$43.0 million. It did not acquire other companies; therefore, it had a fortress like balance sheet with almost no intangible assets, goodwill, or debt.

By comparison to the other large Canadian LPs Cronos has a small operation. Its generated only C$4.1 million in revenue in 2017, C$12.1 million in 2018, C$23.8 million in 2019, and C$46.7 million in 2020. Cronos revenue in 2020 amounted to less than 10% of those reported by Canopy, Tilray, and Aurora. Despite that, Cronos market cap of $3.4 billion was twice Aurora Cannabis $1.7 billion at the end of 2020.

At the end of 2020 Cronos had a C$1.3 billion nest egg of cash and short-term investments. On June 14, 2021 it announced it was spending $110.4 million to acquire an option to buy 10.5% of PharmaCann Inc., a privately held vertically integrated U.S. cannabis company with 23 dispensaries. Like Canopy's deal with Acreage Holdings, the Cronos/PharmaCann deal is contingent on a change in the laws that would allow Cronos to acquire an ownership position.

It is clear Altria has decided how and with whom it wants to enter the U.S. cannabis market. Cronos has the keys to a large vault and none of the baggage of the other large Canadian cannabis companies. It is certain to be a dominant player in the U.S. market if the laws change.

Summary

The six companies presented in this chapter put a spotlight on cannabis as a legitimate sector for investors. Their pioneering efforts established a road map for hundreds of other entrepreneurs to follow. They showed that investors in publicly held companies were willing to invest in foreign companies. The wealth created in the gestation of these six companies drove others to copy the formula.

GW Pharma showed that the road to pharmaceutical riches is long but can be rewarding and that U.S. investors are willing to invest in foreign cannabis companies. Its acquisition illustrates the value of drug discoveries and intellectual property (IP) and how those attributes can overwhelm actual financial results. GW Pharma also demonstrates that cannabis investors expecting quick, vast riches by investing in pharmaceutical companies aiming to develop miracle cures for various diseases are likely to be greatly disappointed.

Stockholders in the five major Canadian cannabis companies expected those companies would earn tremendous profits because of their first-mover advantages. Instead, they have been major financial disappointments for most investor. At their peak stock prices, the five Canadian LPs had a market capitalization of $80.1 billion. As of April 23, 2021 they had a combined market cap of $18.3 billion, down 77.2%.

The large Canadian LPs have left an indelible mark on the cannabis industry by establishing a route from an idea to investor wallets that almost all other cannabis promoters have followed. They used Canada's Business Corporation laws to acquire long dormant public companies via the reverse-takeover (RTO) or amalgamation and then went public on the Canadian Stock Exchange, while keeping a majority of the voting stock in the form of

Super and Multiple Voting Shares. This avenue of going public enabled hundreds of promoters to create publicly held corporations capable of acquiring other entities, while enriching themselves with cheap stock.

The Canadian LPs also took a page out of Canada's rich history of stock speculation by quickly establishing investor relations departments to promote their stocks. People who headed these investor efforts made sure the media knew about the enormous profits likely from cannabis and they swamped the media with press releases. As a result of their efforts, the air waves and print media were awash with tales of imminent great wealth. When Facebook, Twitter, Reddit and other social media cites got caught up in the hype, investor relations became the most important department within cannabis companies. They did such a superb job that into early 2021 the major financial news networks continued to feature the large Canadian cannabis company stocks as if they were the only cannabis stocks in the investment universe.

The above self-promotional efforts coincided with a Canadian investment banking community that was ready, willing, able, and anxious to facilitate the growth of the Canadian cannabis industry, while earning lucrative fees. As a result, IPOs and follow-on offerings were invariably well received by investors anxious to "strike it rich.'

Perhaps the greatest contributing factor to the Canadian LPs being able to attract massive amounts of investor money was the ability of company executives, investment bankers and stockholders to take a page out of ancient Greece where Sophists perfected the use of fallacious arguments with the intent to deceive. As profits and free cash flow failed to materialize, these Canadian stakeholders actively engaged in sophistry by featuring metrics that made a company look good such as square feet under cultivation, revenue, employees, number of products, countries where the company was active, and myriad other metrics that made their results seem better than they were. They absolutely avoided metrics like net income, cash flow, and dilution.

It remains to be seen if these large Canadian companies will ever earn a profit (i.e. net income after taxes) and provide positive cash flow from operations. Until then, they will have to rely on external funding, which is not a problem for Canopy Growth and Cronos, since they have wealthy benefactors in Constellation Brands and Altria. The need for external funding could however be hazardous to stockholders of Aurora Cannabis and the newly merged Tilray.

CHAPTER 2

VERTICALLY INTEGRATED U.S. MARIJUANA COMPANIES

The United States government has been steadfast in maintaining that marijuana is a dangerous drug. Under the Controlled Substances Act, marijuana is listed as a Schedule 1 substance alongside heroin and LSD, which means it has a high potential for abuse and no currently accepted medical use in treatment in the US. Accordingly, interstate transportation of marijuana is illegal and banks, brokerage firms, and stock exchanges are discouraged from doing business with cannabis sector companies.

Despite the Federal government position, legalization of marijuana consumption in the United States emerged in California in 1996 when voters in that state approved Proposition 215 permitting consumer use for medical purposes. In 2012 Colorado and Washington became the first two states to legalize consumption of marijuana for recreational purposes. By June 2021, 18 states plus Washington, DC had legalized recreational consumption, 19 had legalized medical marijuana consumption, and 13 states continued to declare marijuana consumption illegal.

Exhibit 2.1 shows states that permit recreational use of marijuana, those that permit only medical marijuana, and the states where marijuana consumption is illegal. Medical conditions that permit people to consume marijuana differ widely by state. A condition that qualifies in one state may not be a qualifying condition in another. Furthermore, the forms in which the marijuana can be purchased also differ by state. The trend has been for medical marijuana states to fully legalize recreational consumption.

Each state has established unique rules and regulations regarding the cultivation, processing and distribution of marijuana. Most states limited the number of licenses awarded; and, more often than not, those licenses limited the allowable square feet of cultivation and the number of dispensaries that a licensee could operate.

They also listed the form in which marijuana could be dispensed, such that some states prevented the sale of smokable flower or edibles. States also generally allowed municipalities to decide if they would permit cultivation, processing, or distribution in their jurisdiction.

Exhibit 2.1
Marijuana Legal Status By State
(as of June 1, 2021)

Recreational	Medical Only	Illegal
Alaska	Alabama	Georgia
Arizona	Arkansas	Idaho
California	Connecticut	Indiana
Colorado	Delaware	Kansas
Illinois	Florida	Kentucky
Maine	Hawaii	Mississippi
Massachusetts	Iowa	Nebraska
Michigan	Louisiana	North Carolina
Montana	Maryland	South Carolina
New Jersey	Minnesota	Tennessee
New Mexico	Missouri	Texas
New York	North Dakota	Wisconsin
Nevada	Ohio	Wyoming
Oregon	Oklahoma	
South Dakota	New Hampshire	
Vermont	Pennsylvania	
Virginia	Rhode Island	
Washington	Utah	
District of Columbia	West Virginia	

Entrepreneurs

Initial investors in emerging industries or economic sectors tend to reap outsized profits. This is especially true when the number of entrants is limited by law. In such situations there are likely to be a number of applications submitted but only a fortunate few will be awarded licenses.

Early participants in the cannabis industry had to assemble a group of qualified people, submit applications, and get selected before they could begin operations. Once they were awarded licenses, they had to decide on whether they truly had the talent and financial wherewithal to build an enterprise able to grow, process, and/or dispense marijuana. A number of people became applicants in various states as those states began to award licenses, because they knew the licenses alone would be valuable. A significant number of early licensees decided to sell their licenses. Others, especially those who were awarded licenses in more than one state, decided to invest money and become operators.

A Need to Go Public

As licensees began investing in property and equipment they quickly discovered massive amounts of money would be required to fund a seed-to-sale or vertically integrated operating company. That recognition triggered a need to raise substantial amounts of money from investors outside of the initial group members.

Participants quickly realized they needed to take a page out of the game plan used by the Canadian LPs. Accordingly, individuals with significant interests in marijuana licenses hired Canadian investment banking firms to formalize their structures by taking them public on the Canadian Securities Exchange (CSE).

The publicly held marijuana companies currently growing, processing, and distributing product in the United States emerged from the carcasses of dormant CSE mining companies via the RTO/amalgamation process just as Canopy, Aurora, Cronos, Aphria, and Tilray had. In the process of going public the insiders were awarded Super Voting Shares (SVS) and Multiple Voting Shares (MVS) that allowed them to maintain voting control of the company. The companies issued Subordinated Voting Shares at a price per share well above that paid by original investors. Such initial issuance usually left the organizers with at least 80% ownership of the public company and a very, very low-cost basis in their shares.

By offering only a small fraction of the company in the initial public offering, insiders were able to artificially inflate share prices by introducing a scarcity value. At the same time, however, offering a small number of shares did not raise enough money to fund purchases of property and equipment capital and meet the need for working capital.

The fact is that the amount of money raised in these initial offerings was not even close to the amount needed to fund the operations and aspirations of these companies. Accordingly, U.S. cannabis companies had to frequently offer new shares and/or debt obligations in the years after they went public just like their Canadian LP pathfinders.

There is a preconceived belief that the marijuana business offers incredible riches for cultivators, processors, wholesalers, and retailers. Cannabis companies themselves have few peers when it comes to preying on those beliefs. For example, CEOs and IR department heads are quick to point out the total addressable market (TAM) when they enter a new state and the likely size of marijuana sales in a state. Such projections ignore the facts that a company's square feet of cultivation and number of dispensaries are limited and that many municipalities do not permit marijuana operations.

Economies of Scale

The existence of economies of scale is a generally understood and accepted economic principle. Larger companies tend to have lower average costs of production than smaller peers. A basic theorem of microeconomics is if competition is unrestrained, an industry will be dominated by a single large company able to sell products profitably, while smaller companies will be forced out of business because they cannot match the larger company's prices and earn a profit. This fundamental principle is a primary reason companies acquire other companies and the reason for anti-trust laws.

Interestingly, economies of scale do not seem to have worked well enough in Canada to yield profits. Furthermore, they have not been allowed to work in the U.S. because of artificial licensing limitations imposed by various states. Limiting the number of cultivation licenses and/or the square feet of cultivation certainly reduces the supply of cannabis, which tends to cause higher prices. Similarly, a limitation on the number of dispensaries a licensee can operate reduces customer selection tending to cause higher prices.

While license limitations might allow for higher prices, they also deny cost savings that would otherwise be reaped due to economies of scale. Furthermore, intrastate consolidation to achieve economies of scale becomes impossible once participants reach their limits.

The U.S. Multi-State Operator (MSO) Model

The lack of significant economies of scale in a sector dominated by vertical integration has not prevented cannabis CEOs from embracing the multi-state model. A cannabis company that operates in more than one state is known as a multi-state-operator (MSO). In the United States the cannabis companies with the largest market capitalizations are vertically integrated, seed-to-sale MSOs. These companies have been racing each other to establish footprints in limited license states believed to offer rich rewards.

CEOs of MSOs firmly believe that a nationwide footprint and branding will ensure their long run success. That view is supported by a fan club of investment bankers who know that such expansion will require the issuance of a considerable amount of debt and equity.

The fact is that economies of scale vary widely by state and create a situation where certain states may offer little or no profits. This is especially true since companies can only sell in a state what they grow in that state. In that respect, state laws reinforce Federal law by prohibiting the interstate transportation of marijuana.

The current marijuana model is incredibly inefficient. It is the primary cause of high costs, high product prices, and low returns to stock holders. It is as if McDonald stores in Florida could sell only hamburgers and French fries comprised of cattle born, bread, and slaughtered in Florida and potatoes grown there also. Interestingly, the large Canadian companies featured in Chapter 1 do not face the same restrictions; however, they still have been unable earn profits for shareholders.

Cannabis Company Balance Sheet Analysis

Much important information can be gleaned from a careful examination of a cannabis company balance sheet. Among the first and most important things to look at is the cash position of a company relative to its current obligations, which include income taxes payable, current portion of debt payable, and current portion of lease liabilities. These are all serious obligations that require cash. If a company is unable to pay these obligations it runs the risk of lenders forcing a company into bankruptcy and taking possession while wiping out shareholders.

iAnthus Situation

This is exactly what happened at iAnthus when it was unable to pay interest on debentures in March 2020. On April 6, 2020 iAnthus issued a press release announcing it did not make the 13% interest payments totaling $4.4 million due in March 31, 2020 on $159.2 million in debt obligations. iAnthus unsuccessfully attempted to negotiate with the holders of its Secured Debentures for temporary relief of interest payments.

Incredibly, the press release announcing the default also said "the Company will continue to pursue expansion opportunities in retail, cultivation and manufacturing, as well as further development of its retail and product brands. Deploying these efforts with a ruthless focus on the customer experience and the patient journey, iAnthus remains committed to its mission to create the most valuable cannabis brands and network of cannabis operations and distribution nationally." This hubris failed to comfort shareholders who dumped iAnthus shares.

The day prior to the default announcement ITHUF closed at $0.4690 per share on the OTC with volume of 279,000 shares. On the day of the announcement 8 million shares traded and iAnthus stock closed down 61.6% at $0.179.

iAnthus continued to remain in default on its debt obligation and as of March 31, 2021. On that date it owed $25 million in past due interest payments on debentures along with $157.5 million in principal. Additionally, it accrued fees and interest of $14.2 million as a result of its default.

As of mid year 2021 iAnthus was in the process of being recapitalized. As expected, the plan of recapitalization has been designed by debt holders. Among other things, it involves the issuance of up to 6,072,579,699 shares of common stock in exchange for debt extinguishment. As of March 31, 2021 there were 171,718,192 iAnthus shares outstanding; therefore, existing shareholders, who currently own 100% of iAnthus will end up owning only 2.75% (171,718,192/6,244,297,891) of iAnthus. A number of observers believe that iAnthus is the "canary in the coal mine."

iAnthus stock (ITHUF) closed at $0.189 on June 30, 2021. That price equates to a pro forma market capitalization of $1.18 billion based on a recapitalized iAnthus having 6,244,297,891 shares outstanding. That would make it about the 15th largest U.S. MSO.

Income Taxes Payable

Exhibit 2.2 shows the cash adequacy of 35 U.S. cannabis companies. Income tax payable, current portion of debt due, and current portion of lease liabilities are each expressed as a percentage company cash as reported in audited balance sheets for the year ended December 31, 2020. The three are then totaled to give an overall measure of cash adequacy.

Exhibit 2.2
Adequacy of U.S. Cannabis Company Cash Positions
(December 31, 2020)

Company	Symbol	Income Taxes Payable	Current Debt Payable	Current Lease Liabilities	Total
Curaleaf	CURLF	108.3%	8.8%	21.4%	138.5%
Green Thumb	GTBIF	19.3%	0.4%	4.6%	24.3%
Trulieve	TCNNF	4.0%	9.5%	4.8%	18.3%
Verano Holdings	VRNOF	152.2%	30.8%	9.7%	192.7%
Cresco Labs	CRLBF	36.2%	11.0%	18.1%	65.4%
Terrascend	TRSSF	46.8%	9.7%	2.9%	59.4%
Columbia Care	CCHWF	0.0%	13.8%	16.3%	30.1%
Harvest Health	HRVSF	22.4%	26.8%	3.9%	53.1%
Chalice Brands Ltd	CHALF	110.9%	631.6%	104.9%	847.4%
Planet 13	PLNHF	1.5%	1.1%	0.0%	2.7%
Ayr Wellness	AYRWF	17.0%	6.8%	0.7%	24.4%
Ascend Wellness	AAWH	32.3%	104.9%	3.8%	141.0%
Jushi Holdings	JUSHF	19.9%	1.6%	5.5%	26.9%
4Front Ventures	FFNTF	60.8%	26.5%	10.1%	97.4%
Acreage Holdings	ACRHF	45.4%	83.4%	4.6%	133.4%
Goodness Holdings	GDNSF	28.3%	7.9%	0.0%	36.2%
Item 9 Labs	INLB	0.0%	275.4%	3.7%	279.2%
Gage Growth Corp	GAEGF	2.9%	7.4%	2.2%	12.5%
MariMed	MRMD	0.0%	376.1%	34.9%	411.0%
Tilt Holdings	TLLTF	1.0%	62.9%	21.7%	85.6%
MedMen	MMNFF	1143.6%	279.9%	86.1%	1509.7%
Cansortium	CNTMF	263.1%	1137.5%	55.8%	1456.4%
Red White & Bloom	RWBYF	272.6%	5883.9%	18.0%	6174.4%
C21 Investments	CXXIF	54.2%	137.9%	7.0%	199.0%
Next Green Wave	NXGWF	0.0%	67.3%	0.9%	68.2%
Stem Holdings	STMH	0.0%	323.5%	27.0%	350.5%
Harborside	HBORF	70.6%	4.5%	4.7%	79.8%
Medicine Man	SHWZ	0.0%	406.1%	0.0%	406.1%
Lowell Farms	LOWLF	0.0%	4.7%	8.9%	13.6%
Slang Worldwide	SLGWF	0.0%	57.4%	5.1%	62.5%
Vibe Growth	VBSCF	82.5%	7.9%	12.8%	103.2%
Hollister Bio	HSTRF	73.2%	78.3%	79.8%	231.3%
Body & Mind	BMMJ	299.3%	4.7%	37.9%	341.9%
iAnthus Capital	ITHUF	0.0%	1425.7%	67.6%	1493.3%
Plus Products	PLPRF	0.0%	167.2%	2.1%	169.3%

Having the current liability "income tax payable" by itself is not a sign of weakness, since the U.S. Treasury penalty for nonpayment at the present time is 6% per annum, which is well below the interest rate at which most cannabis companies can borrow money. An air of excitement would certainly be created if the IRS put a lien on the assets of a publicly held cannabis company and took control.

It conjures up visions of bygone days when the Federal Deposit Insurance Corporation (FDIC) was rumored to have taken control the Mustang Ranch, a famous brothel in Sparks, Nevada. The truth is the FDIC never did take control. The Mustang Ranch was actually operated by a Bankruptcy Trustee appointed by the United States Bankruptcy Court on behalf of the United States Government.

Exhibit 2.2 shows income tax payable exceeded available cash at six U.S. companies. The company that depended the most on the nonpayment of taxes for cash at the end of 2020 was MedMen.

Its taxes payable equaled 1,143.6% of its cash (11.44x its cash position). Other companies that had taxes payable greater than their cash were Body and Mind at 299.3%, Cansortium at 263.1%, Verano Holdings at 152.2%, Chalice Brands at 110.9%, and Curaleaf at 108.3%.

Current Portion of Debt Payable

At the end of 2020 the current portion of debt payable exceeded the cash position at 11 of the 35 cannabis companies. Notably the company with the worst cash position was iAnthus with debt due equal to 1,425.7% of its cash. The current portion of iAnthus debt exceeded its cash by 14.3x. It is not surprising that it defaulted on its debt obligations and lost control of the company to its creditors. Other companies that had more current debt than cash were Cansortium at 1,137.5%, Chalice Brands at 631.6%, Medicine Man at 406.1%, Mari Med at 376.1%, Stem Holdings at 323.5%, MedMen at 279.9%, Item 9 Labs at 275.4%, Plus Products at 167.2%, C21 Investments at 137.9%, and Ascend Wellness at 104.9%.

It is not surprising that the auditor for iAnthus issued a qualified opinion that accompanied its 2020 annual audit. It stated that the financial statements were prepared assuming that iAnthus would continue as a going concern; however, it said iAnthus had a significant working capital deficiency, had incurred significant losses and needed to raise additional funds to meet its obligations and sustain its operations. The auditor letter went on to say that aforementioned conditions raise substantial doubt about the ability of iAnthus to continue as a going concern. Similar qualified opinions by auditors of other cannabis companies could have been written but were not.

Current Lease Liabilities

At the end of 2020 the current portion of lease liabilities alone did not appear to require as much cash. The only companies with relatively larger percentage of cash going toward current lease payments were Chalice Brands at 104.9%, MedMen at 86.1%, Hollister Biosciences at 79.8%, iAnthus at 67.6%, and Cansortium at 55.8%.

Exhibit 2.2 shows that once the current obligations are combined only about half of the U.S. companies had a sufficient amount of cash to comfortably meet those obligations. Ten of the companies had current obligation that exceeded twice the amount of cash they had available. The company with the worst cash adequacy was MedMen. Its current obligations were 15.1x its cash. It was followed by iAnthus at 14.9x, Cansortium at 14.6x, Chalice Brands at 8.5x, Mari Med at 4.1x, and Medicine Man also at 4.1x.

This examination of cash positions reveals that U.S. cannabis companies were not flush with cash at the end of 2020. In fact, it suggests that a significant number ended 2020 with a dire need for cash. Such a need led iAnthus into the clutches of creditors, while others have been forced to scramble for cash. A number of companies were known to be offering to pay bills with shares of stock to preserve cash in 2020.

Accumulated Deficit

Any analysis of a cannabis company balance sheet must include a review of the equity position. Among other items shown in the equity section of a cannabis company balance sheet is "accumulated deficit." The amount shown in this equity category is the amount of money a company has lost since it opened for business.

If a company continually loses money its equity capital will diminish to the point where lenders and investors will become concerned about the possibility of failure. A company with negative equity, liabilities greater than assets, is insolvent on the basis of its balance sheet and a candidate for Chapter 7 bankruptcy. The belief that new companies in new industries always lose money is a worn-out mantra used by floundering cannabis companies to explain their failings and should not be accepted by investors.

Losses in the early years of some businesses are understandable. For example, a biopharmaceutical company established to develop a cure for a disease might spend many years trying to discover that cure. If the company discovered a cure it would then have to be tested in numerous trials over a period of years before receiving the necessary regulatory approvals. Only then could the drug be sold and revenue start flowing.

GW Pharma, which was discussed earlier, is a classic example of the gestation period of a drug discovery. The biopharmaceutical area is probably the best example of a sector where large persistent losses can accumulate for an extended period of time. It is a sector that offers great rewards to investors in those few companies that discover a cure. It is also a sector where unlimited amounts of investor dollars can be lost without any sales ever being generated.

Investors need to be extremely cautious about investing in a cannabis company that promotes itself as a biopharmaceutical company. They are either hopeful this will help their stock valuation or they are delusional.

Another example of a business where early losses can be expected seems appropriate. If investors wanted to start an orange grove from scratch, they would need land which would need prepared for planting. They would then need seedlings to transplant. Those seedlings would then have to be cared for until they started to bear fruit which would likely be 4-5 years after planting before the first crop of oranges was harvested. Needless to say, investors in this orange grove should expect to lose money for 4-5 years.

The time it takes for a major biopharmaceutical discovery is far more indeterminant than the time it takes to grow trees or raise livestock. A farmer who grows crops does not expect to lose money for a period of years.

Investors in a cannabis company should not accept the statement that consistent annual losses are typical and should be expected during the early years. The fact is that it takes only a fraction of a year to produce a crop of cannabis.

It is not surprising that Trulieve, a cannabis company started by nurserymen whose ancestors grew shade tobacco, could turn a profit in its first year of operation. It is also not surprising that cannabis companies organized and run by Wall Street financiers continually lose money, since they probably never potted a plant or herb.

Exhibit 2.3 shows that accumulated deficits of 35 U.S. cannabis companies from their inception through December 31, 2020. Interestingly, the accumulated deficits totaled $6.2 billion, and the total equity of all was $6.1 billion at the end of 2020. So, since these companies formed they have lost as much as they currently show in equity!

Only two of the 35 companies show an accumulated gain since their formation. Those companies are Trulieve and Gage Growth Corporation. Through the end of 2020 Trulieve had an accumulated profit of $120 million, while Gage growth reported a gain of 473 million. Companies reporting the largest accumulated losses were Tilt Holdings at $800 million, iAnthus at $721 million, MedMen at $674 million, Acreage Holdings at $475 million, and Ayr Wellness at $428 million.

Intangible Assets and Goodwill

Most of the integrated U.S. cannabis companies have been formed by publicly held companies buying other companies and by owners of non-public cannabis companies rolling-up their ownership interests and going public in an IPO. Both types of formation give rise to large amounts of "goodwill" and "intangible assets" that are generally considered non-earning assets. In any acquisition or company formation the hard assets like land, plant and equipment are valued along with intangible assets like licenses, tradenames, customer relationships, non-compete agreements, and trademarks.

Exhibit 2.3
Accumulated Deficit and Financial Leverage
(December 31, 2020)

Company	Symbol	Accumulated Deficit	Total Liabilities as Percentage of Equity	Total Liabilities as Percentage of Tangible Equity
Curaleaf	CURLF	-194,645,000	73.4%	929.8%
Green Thumb	GTBIF	-145,498,623	48.6%	354.9%
Trulieve	TCNNF	119,690,000	82.2%	129.8%
Verano Holdings	VRNOF	0	62.7%	81.4%
Cresco Labs	CRLBF	-286,197,000	83.9%	786.2%
Terrascend	TRSSF	-316,696,154	5332.1%	-661.9%
Columbia Care	CCHWF	-304,603,000	146.2%	530.5%
Harvest Health	HRVSF	-293,607,000	128.8%	-3523.5%
Chalice Brands Ltd	CHALF	-150,683,854	412.0%	-241.9%
Planet 13	PLNHF	-28,986,212	24.3%	31.3%
Ayr Wellness	AYRWF	-427,612,883	308.2%	-239.9%
Ascend Wellness	AAWH	-63,592,000	11198.2%	-610.3%
Jushi Holdings	JUSHF	-264,091,000	-203082.5%	-220.2%
4Front Ventures	FFNTF	-250,548,000	385.2%	-1668.6%
Acreage Holdings	ACRHF	-475,205,000	133.2%	457.8%
Goodness Holdings	GDNSF	-101,733,044	64.6%	79.3%
Item 9 Labs	INLB	-24,042,778	96.8%	288.7%
Gage Growth Corp	GAEGF	72,684,693	116.9%	117.3%
MariMed	MRMD	-104,616,538	843.7%	1163.9%
Tilt Holdings	TLLTF	-800,074,000	51.8%	261.8%
MedMen	MMNFF	-674,420,245	203.9%	-19389.1%
Cansortium	CNTMF	-138,988,000	455.2%	-179.1%
Red White & Bloom	RWBYF	-25,580,378	109.6%	456.6%
C21 Investments	CXXIF	-76,616,401	171.6%	-307.0%
Next Green Wave	NXGWF	-16,080,380	19.5%	19.5%
Stem Holdings	STMH	-54,574,000	57.8%	-373.9%
Harborside	HBORF	-92,257,217	517.1%	-179.6%
Medicine Man	SHWZ	-42,293,098	69.2%	-201.4%
Lowell Farms	LOWLF	-79,416,000	143.7%	147.1%
Slang Worldwide	SLGWF	-191,047,939	61.2%	-822.9%
Vibe Growth	VBSCF	-11,388,774	81.4%	230.7%
Hollister Bio	HSTRF	-7,633,129	192.4%	1369.2%
Body & Mind	BMMJ	-16,853,054	26.7%	133.7%
iAnthus Capital	ITHUF	-720,629,000	604.1%	-284.5%

When the acquisition price exceeds the assigned value of all real and intangible assets acquired, the difference is identified as goodwill. Intangible assets are written off as expenses through the income statement over a period of years, while goodwill is not written off. Intangible assets and goodwill are supposedly subjected to regular tests to determine if there is any impairment under an income approach whereby fair value is based on the present value of estimated future cash flows.

Intangible assets are generally amortized as an expense through the income statement on a straight-line method over the estimated useful lives of the asset. It is typical that licenses be amortized over 15 years, tradenames over 2-10 years, customer relationships over 5 years, non-compete agreements over the life of the agreements, and trademarks over 6 months to 1 year.

Impairment Charge Threat

The prior chapter noted that Aurora Cannabis was forced by its auditors to write-off C$2.8 billion in goodwill and intangibles because of impairment. That write-off occurred because the auditors determined Aurora had simply paid way too much for acquisitions that proved worthless and the goodwill they booked as an asset was meritless.

Some observers suggest the Aurora write-offs should have occurred much sooner. They also believe the same fate awaits U.S. MSOs which are littering the asset side of their balance sheets with large amounts of intangible assets and goodwill. In particular, there is a growing belief that the intrinsic value of licenses and goodwill will plummet as the states increase number of issued licenses.

Intrinsic values will also plummet if the Federal government removes its prohibition on interstate transportation of cannabis. If cannabis could be freely transported across state lines, huge cannabis cultivation sites would be constructed in areas that offered the greatest advantages for quality and yield at the lowest cost.

Companies with high cost, older, less efficient cannabis cultivation facilities would be seriously disadvantaged. At the same time, Amazon like companies could reduce the need for dispensaries, since cannabis products could be readily delivered overnight.

Tangible Equity Capital

Because of the problems associated with valuing intangible assets and goodwill, the reported equity capital of a cannabis company needs to be adjusted. In particular, any determination of capital adequacy needs to reduce the amount of equity capital by the amount of intangible assets and goodwill. Tangible equity capital is a better measure of capital adequacy and is calculated by subtracting intangible assets and goodwill from reported equity capital.

In prior decades stock market investors relied heavily on the book value of a stock to make investment decisions. While that has fallen out of favor in recent years, book value and especially tangible book value gained many followers among bank stock investors in the wake of the Lehman Brothers and Bear Stearns collapses.

Increasing concern has been expressed that the current era of low interest rates and readily available money has fostered the use of increased financial leverage by all companies. Low rates have certainly not been available to cannabis companies, which have consistently had to pay double digit rates of interest to borrow money. Despite those high rates cannabis companies have managed to leverage their balance sheet to lofty levels.

Exhibit 2.3 shows the degree of financial leverage employed by 35 cannabis companies by expressing their total liabilities as percentage of their equity and tangible equity capital. As of the end of 2020, Jushi Holdings was the most levered based on total liabilities to equity since its balance sheet showed its equity was a negative $177,000.

Among the other cannabis companies, the highest total liabilities to equity ratios were reported by Plus Products at 429x, Ascend Wellness at 112x, Terrascend at 53x, Mari Med at 8x, iAnthus at 6x, and Harborside at 5x.

When financial leverage is measured relative to tangible equity, which excludes intangibles and goodwill, the degrees of financial leverage explode. In fact, tangible equity at the end of 2020 was negative for 15 of the companies presented in Exhibit 2.3. The lowest degrees of financial leverage based on the ratio of total liabilities to tangible equity were recorded by Next Green Wave at 19.5%, Planet 13 at 31.3%, Goodness Holdings at 79.3% and Verano at 81.4%.

Cannabis Company Income Statement Analysis

Investors who intend to buy publicly held cannabis company stocks need to know how to read a company income statement. With that thought in mind, Exhibit 2.4 is the 2020 audited annual Statement of Operations and Income of Trulieve, which is a U.S. MSO. Exhibit 2.4 is typical of cannabis companies that prepare their financial statements based on generally accepted accounting principles (GAAP).

The Trulieve income statement is presented in U.S. dollars and begins with total revenue net of any discounts of $521,533,000 and excise/sales taxes. Costs of goods sold of $135,116,000 are then deducted to arrive at gross profit of $386,418,000.

Companies that prepare their financial statements on the basis of International Financial Reporting Standard (IFRS) principles generally show a gross profit figure before the gain or loss in biologicals and another gross profit figure after considering the impact of biologicals. Trulieve converted from using IFRS to GAAP in 2020 when it decided to start reporting to the United States Securities and Exchange Commission (SEC). It therefore no longer reports the unrealized fair value gain on growth of biologicals or the realized fair value amounts included in inventory sold that are required under IFRS.

Regardless of accounting principles, Exhibit 2.4 shows that operating expenses ($168,051,000) which include general and administrative expenses ($36,056,000), sales and marketing expenses ($119,395,000), and depreciation and amortization ($12,600,000) are deducted from gross profit to arrive at income from operations, which amounts to $218,367,000 and is known as net operating income.

Other non-operating expenses of $60,917,000 which includes net interest expense of $20,237,000 and other net expenses of $40,680,000 are then deducted to arrive at net income before taxes of $157,450,000. Taxes of $94,451,000 which include current taxes of $99,338,000 and a deferred tax credit of $4,887,000 are then deducted to yield net income after taxes of $62,999,000.

Exhibit 2.4
Trulieve Cannabis Corporation
Statement of Operations And Income: 2020
(US dollars)

Net Revenues	521,533,000
Cost of Goods Sold	135,116,000
Gross Profit	386,418,000
Operating Expenses:	
General and Administrative	36,056,000
Sales and Marketing	119,395,000
Depreciation and Amortization	12,600,000
Total Operating Expenses	168,051,000
Income from Operations	218,367,000
Other Income (Expense)	
Interest Expense, Net	(20,237,000)
Other (Expense) Income, Net	(40,680,000)
Total Other Expense	(60,917,000)
Net Income Before Taxes	157,450,000
Current Income Taxes	99,338,000
Deferred Income Tax	(4,887,000)
Net Income After Taxes	62,999,000

The fact that Trulieve actually had a current income tax liability of $99,338,000 or 63.1% of its net income before taxes is noteworthy. The astronomically high effective tax rate is an anchor around the neck of the cannabis industry. It exists because cannabis companies are only allowed to deduct expenses directly attributable to growing cannabis plants. All expenses such as advertising, marketing, bad debts, board meeting expenses, business association dues, vehicle expenses, charitable deductions, legal fees, office supplies, payroll processing, payroll taxes for employees (including Social Security, Medicare and unemployment taxes), parking, tolls, sales staff salaries and wages, equipment and repairs, furniture and fixtures, rent, home office expenses, insurance premiums, shipping costs, computer software and equipment, utilities, website, workers compensation, and many more things are not deductible for tax purposes. If Trulieve was treated like other corporations it would have saved $50,646,000 in taxes in 2020 and its net income after taxes would have been $113,645,000 or 80.4% higher that what it reported!

Net income after taxes is what is earned by the owners of a cannabis company after all earned revenue and known expenses have been recognized. Lenders and investors prefer companies that consistently earn profits, especially companies that grow their profits.

Importance of Margin

When gross profit is expressed as a percentage of revenue it is called gross profit margin. The gross profit margins of companies within the cannabis industry can be compared to help determine which company has the lowest cost of cultivation.

Similarly, expressing operating expenses as a percentage of net revenue provides a gauge of operating efficiency and is referred to as the operating expense ratio. More efficient cannabis companies will have lower ratios.

When net operating income is expressed as a percentage of net revenue the quotient is referred to as the net operating margin. If the gross profit margin exceeds the operating expense ratio then the company has net operating income and a positive net operating income margin. If the gross profit margin is less than the operating expense ratio then the company has a net operating loss and a negative net operating income margin.

Margin Analysis of U.S. Cannabis Companies

Exhibit 2.5 shows the gross profit margin, operating expense ratio, and net operating margin for 36 vertically integrated cannabis companies operating in the United States in 2020. The impact of biological assets has been excluded from this analysis to facilitate a proper comparison between companies using IFRS and those using GAAP accounting. The companies are listed in descending order of their market capitalizations as of March 31, 2021.

Gross Profit Margin

Trulieve has, by far, the highest gross profit margin of any of the cannabis companies in Exhibit 2.5. Its gross profit margin of 74.1% dwarfs all other vertically integrated cannabis companies. Its outsized margin is a tribute to economies of scale arising from it having two million square feet of cultivation in northwest Florida. Trulieve also benefits from it being located in the Quincy, Florida area, where land and labor costs are relatively low. It has also benefited from being founded by three nurserymen with years of cultivation experience.

The company with the next highest gross margin was 4Front Ventures at 63.3%, more than 1000 basis points (100 basis points equals 1%) away. Other company's in the top five included Verano at 63.1%, MariMed at 61.5%, and Cansortium at 59.9%.

Companies with five lowest gross profit margins in 2020 were Hollister Biosciences 10.2%, Lowell Farms 10.6%, Body and Mind 22.3%, Stem Holdings 26.2%, and Gage Growth 27.1%.

Gross profit margin is a closely followed metric that merits investor attention. A movement as small as 100 basis points, such as an increase in gross margin from 50% to 51%, amounts to millions of dollars for large MSOs that have more than $100 million in net annual revenue.

Exhibit 2.5
U.S. Company Operating Margins: 2020

Company	Symbol	Gross Profit	Operating Expenses	Operating Income
Curaleaf	CURLF	50.3%	52.2%	-1.9%
Green Thumb	GTBIF	54.7%	35.6%	19.1%
Trulieve	TCNNF	74.1%	32.2%	41.9%
Verano Holdings	VRNOF	63.1%	24.0%	39.1%
Cresco Labs	CRLBF	43.2%	47.9%	-4.7%
Terrascend	TRSSF	54.6%	43.1%	11.5%
Columbia Care	CCHWF	36.6%	78.0%	-41.4%
Harvest Health	HRVSF	43.9%	58.6%	-14.7%
Chalice Brands Ltd	CHALF	32.0%	56.3%	-24.3%
Planet 13	PLNHF	48.5%	49.1%	-0.6%
Ayr Wellness	AYRWF	57.1%	56.1%	1.0%
Ascend Wellness	AAWH	42.4%	36.9%	5.5%
Jushi Holdings	JUSHF	45.3%	64.3%	-19.1%
4Front Ventures	FFNTF	63.3%	119.9%	-56.6%
Acreage Holdings	ACRHF	42.9%	361.4%	-318.5%
Goodness Holdings	GDNSF	34.8%	81.6%	-46.8%
Item 9 Labs	INLB	44.1%	91.7%	-47.7%
Gage Growth Corp	GAEGF	27.1%	87.2%	-60.1%
MariMed	MRMD	61.5%	33.0%	28.5%
Tilt Holdings	TLLTF	29.5%	59.1%	-29.6%
MedMen	MMNFF	46.3%	309.4%	-263.1%
Cansortium	CNTMF	59.9%	73.1%	-13.2%
Red White & Bloom	RWBYF	59.4%	206.9%	-147.5%
C21 Investments	CXXIF	46.0%	30.0%	16.0%
Next Green Wave	NXGWF	41.7%	28.5%	13.2%
Stem Holdings	STMH	26.2%	95.4%	-69.2%
Harborside	HBORF	44.2%	52.5%	-8.3%
Medicine Man	SHWZ	28.2%	123.7%	-95.5%
Lowell Farms	LOWLF	10.6%	48.3%	-37.7%
Slang Worldwide	SLGWF	47.7%	132.9%	-85.2%
Vibe Growth	VBSCF	33.8%	26.9%	6.9%
Hollister Bio	HSTRF	10.2%	20.9%	-1.9%
Body & Mind	BMMJ	22.3%	40.5%	-1.9%
iAnthus Capital	ITHUF	57.2%	218.7%	-161.6%
Plus Products	PLPRF	35.4%	87.7%	-52.3%

Operating Expense Ratio

The company with the lowest operating expense ratio in Exhibit 2.5 was Hollister Biosciences, whose operating expenses amounted to only 20.9% of its revenue. It was followed by Verano at 24%, Vibe Growth at 26.9%, Next Green Wave at 28.5%, C21 Investments at 30%, and Trulieve at 32.2%.

The company that recorded the worst operating expense ratio in 2020 was Acreage Holdings, which had operating expenses that amounted to 361.4% of its revenue. It was closely followed by MedMen at 309.4%.

Others with embarrassing operating expense ratios were IAnthus Capital at 218.7%, Slang Worldwide at 132.9%, Medicine Man at 123.7%, and 4Front Ventures at 119.9%.

Net Operating Margin

Ten of the companies shown in Exhibit 2.5 had positive net operating income margins. The company with the largest net operating margin was Trulieve, which had a net operating margin of 41.9%. It was followed by Verano at 39.1%, MariMed at 28.5%, C21 Investments at 16.0%, Next Green Wave at 13.2%, and Terrascend at 11.5%.

Of the 26 companies that recorded negative net operating margins, five stood out. The net operating loss of Acreage Holdings was 318.5% of its revenue. That poor performance was followed closely by MedMen at 263.1% then by iAnthus at 161.6%, Medicine Man at 95.5%, and Slang Worldwide at 85.2%.

Margin Analysis of Canada's Big Five

The five large Canadian cannabis companies were also examined to see how their gross profit margins, operating expense ratios, and net operating profit margins compared to U.S. cannabis companies. The result of that comparable analysis for their most recent twelve months is presented in Exhibit 2.6.

Exhibit 2.6
Canadian Company Operating Margins: 2020

Company	Symbol	Gross Profit	Operating Expenses	Operating Income
Canopy Growth	CGC	18.3%	249.9%	-231.6%
Aphria	APHA	26.6%	47.7%	-21.1%
Tilray	TLRY	11.7%	107.3%	-95.6%
Cronos	CRON	0.5%	328.6%	-328.1%
Aurora Cannabis	ACB	48.6%	116.4%	-67.8%

It is hard to believe that the supposed leading companies in the industry that have been in business for at least six years could produce such horrible numbers. These are the same companies that provided the template being followed by U. S. cannabis companies.

The gross profit margin of Aurora Cannabis at 48.6% and the operating expense ratio of Aphria at 47.7% are somewhat respectable. The rest of the percentages for gross profit margin, operating expense ratio, and net operating margin are incredibly bad. They rank with the worst of the U.S. companies presented in Exhibit 2.5.

The individual results reported by Tilray and Aphria were combined to gain some perspective on what might be expected following their merger. Their combined pro forma results show a low gross profit margin of 22.7%, a high operating expense ratio of 63.1%, and a significant negative net operating margin at 40.4% of net revenue.

Cannabis Company Profitability

Only six of the 10 U.S. companies with positive net operating margins reported profits in 2020. None of the top five Canadian companies reported any net income after taxes.

Return on equity (ROE) is a preferred way to measure profitability. Applying that measure to the six profitable companies that operated throughout 2020 revealed that Mari Med had the highest ROE at 29.99%. The second most profitable company was Next Green Wave which had an ROE of 20.35%. It was followed by Body & Mind at 14.08%, Trulieve at 14.07%, Vibe Growth at 7.21%, and Green Thumb at 1.65%.

A double-digit ROE at a time when the risk-free U.S. Treasury bond rate is hovering around 3% is really quite good. By comparison, Microsoft has an ROE of 45%, Proctor & Gamble 30.7%, Facebook 28%, Merck 26%, Google 25%, Walmart 15.7%, and JP Morgan 15% in 2020.

Cannabis Company Cash Flow Analysis

Quarterly financial statements filed by publicly held cannabis companies with the SEC or SEDAR include a Statements of Cash Flows. Exhibit 2.7 is the cash flow statement filed by Ayr Wellness in its audited annual report for 2020.

The cash flow statement is divided into three important sections. Normally, the first section begins with net profit after taxes as reported on the income statement. Ayr Wellness, however, reported a net loss after taxes on its income statement for 2020 of $176,332,658, therefore, its statements of cash flows begins with that reported net loss.

Its net loss is then adjusted to account for noncash expenses recognized in its income statement. Those noncash expenses include the net fair value loss on financial liabilities of $164,042,264; stock-based compensation of $31,156,759; depreciation of $4,720,198; amortization of intangible assets of $13,716,502; share of unrealized loss on equity investments of $33,591; deferred tax expense of $2,388,608; amortization of financing costs of $90,858; and interest accrued of $2,214,061.

Changes in assets and liabilities that provided cash or used cash were then included in Section 1 of the Ayr statements of cash flows. Increases in assets are a use of cash, therefore, accounts receivable grew by $843,162 in 2020 and used that amount of cash; inventory and biological assets growth required $8,876,748 in cash; and the growth in prepaid expenses and other assets used $2,529,212 in cash.

Exhibit 2.7
Ayr Wellness Statements of Cash Flows for 2020

Operating Activities	
Net Income (Loss) After taxes	$ (176,332,658)
Adjustments for:	
Net fair value loss on financial liabilities	164,042,264
Stock-based compensation	31,156,759
Depreciation	4,720,198
Amortization of intangible assets	13,716,502
Share of loss on equity investments	33,591
Fair value adjustment on sale of inventory	34,147,938
Unrealized gain on biological asset transformation	(48,690,657)
Deferred tax expense (benefit)	2,388,608
Amortization on financing costs	90,858
Interest accrued	2,214,061
Changes in non-cash operations, net of business acquisition	
Accounts receivable	(843,162)
Inventory and biological assets	(8,876,748)
Prepaid expenses and other assets	(2,529,212)
Trade payables	1,616,253
Accrued liabilities	3,274,488
Income tax payable	16,382,580
Cash Provided by Operating Activities	36,511,663
Investing Activities	
Purchase of property, plant and equipment	(14,367,690)
Purchases of intangible assets	(400,000)
Cash paid for business combinations and asset acquisitions, net of cash acquired	(35,174,880)
Cash paid for business combinations and asset acquisitions, bridge financing	(8,040,804)
Cash paid for business combinations and asset acquisitions, working capital	(2,354,375)
Payments for interests in equity accounted investments	(109,700)
Advances to related corporation	(50,000)
Deposits for business combinations	(1,750,000)
Cash (used in) provided by investing activities	(62,247,449)
Financing Activities	
Proceeds from exercise of warrants	48,483,750
Proceeds from senior secured notes, net of financing costs	103,571,105
Repayments of debts payable	(5,615,225)
Repayments of lease obligation (principal portion)	(1,557,445)
Repurchase of Subordinate Voting Shares	(311,430)
Cash provided by (used in) financing activities	144,570,755
Net Increase in Cash	118,834,969
Cash and cash equivalents, beginning of the year	8,403,196
Cash and cash equivalents, end of year	127,238,165

Increases in liabilities are sources of cash in Section 1 of the statements of cash flow. Exhibit 2.7 shows Ayr trade payables increased by $1,616,253 providing cash; accrued liabilities increased by $3,274,488 providing cash; and income tax payable increased by $16,382,580 providing cash.

Exhibit 2.7 shows that after taking into consideration income, expenses, and changes in working capital, Ayr had cash provided from operation in 2020 of $36,511,663. The remainder of the cash flow statement is divided into Investing Activities and Financing Activities. Ayr used $62,247,449 in investment activities and it acquired $144,570,000 from financing activities.

The Ayr Statements of Cash Flows, Exhibit 2.7, shows that cash provided by operating activities was $36,511,663 despite a net loss after taxes reported on its income statement of $176,332,658. At the same time, it tapped the financial markets for $144,570,755, while it invested $62,247,449. These various cash flow figures raise the question: What is the cash flow of AYR Wellness?

Free Cash Flow

What is the cash flow of Ayr wellness? Is it the cash provided from operating activities, which was $36.5 million? It is the amount by which cash on the balance sheet increased during 2020, which was $118.8 million, which is the sum of the cash provided from operating activities, $36.5 million, plus the cash provided by financing activities, $144.6 million, minus the cash used in investing activities, $62.3 million?

It is essential that cash flow be properly defined and measured. After all, modern corporate finance is built of the premise that the value of any business is the discounted present value of the cash that owners of a business receive from operating the business. Cash that is paid out to owners must be over and above the cash needed to properly run a business including paying all bills in a timely fashion.

These considerations give rise to the concept of "free" cash flow, which can be defined as the amount of cash provided by company operating activities less any current income taxes not paid during a given period of time. Cannabis companies have artificially inflated their cash flow by not paying current income taxes. For example, $11,179,637 of the $16,382,580 in income tax payable on the Ayr statement of cash flow was income tax it incurred but did not pay in 2020. When that is taken into consideration, the free cash flow of Ayr becomes $25,332,026, which is 30.6% below its reported cash provided by operating activities.

Exhibit 2.8 shows a comparison of cash flow provided from operating activities and free cash flow (as defined above) for 35 U.S. cannabis companies. The cash provided by operations (column 1) at all 35 companies totaled $81.8 million, ranging from a positive net operating cash flow at Verano of $150.8 million to a negative $81.0 million at MedMen. Only 12 (34.2%) of the 35 companies shown in Exhibit 2.8 reported positive net operating cash flow in 2020.

Column 2 in Exhibit 2.8 shows the amounts of current income taxes companies incurred in 2020 but did not pay. The income taxes these companies did not pay totaled $320.5 million. MedMen was responsible for incurring the largest amount of unpaid taxes, $59.8 million.

When the nonpayment of income taxes is factored into a discussion of cash flow, it becomes clear that the amount reported on GAAP Statements of Cash Flows is not a perfect measure. In fact, it falls far short of the cash flow figure required in generally accepted valuation analysis.

Exhibit 2.8
Company Free Cash Flow for 2020

Company	Symbol	Cash From Operations	2020 Tax Not Paid	Free Cash Flow
Curaleaf	CURLF	12,355,000	57,753,000	-45,398,000
Green Thumb	GTBIF	95,916,965	8,540,102	87,376,863
Trulieve	TCNNF	99,643,000	-2,452,000	102,095,000
Verano Holdings	VRNOF	150,773,720	35,876,195	114,897,525
Cresco Labs	CRLBF	-10,831,000	34,213,000	-45,044,000
Terrascend	TRSSF	25,394,615	10,801,538	14,593,077
Columbia Care	CCHWF	-42,606,000	-1,913,000	-40,693,000
Harvest Health	HRVSF	-31,549,000	12,194,000	-43,743,000
Chalice Brands Ltd	CHALF	-1,456,771	1,003,604	-2,460,375
Planet 13	PLNHF	-914,965	-5,794,954	4,879,989
Ayr Wellness	AYRWF	36,511,663	16,382,580	20,129,083
Ascend Wellness	AAWH	-6,004,000	14,725,000	-20,729,000
Jushi Holdings	JUSHF	-3,720,000	14,586,000	-18,306,000
4Front Ventures	FFNTF	-13,414,000	9,893,000	-23,307,000
Acreage Holdings	ACRHF	-67,678,000	10,040,000	-77,718,000
Goodness Holdings	GDNSF	-10,932,383	6,782,934	-17,715,317
Item 9 Labs	INLB	-2,750,820	-87,476	-2,663,344
Gage Growth Corp	GAEGF	-12,373,916	1,324,114	-13,698,030
MariMed	MRMD	3,380,303	0	3,380,303
Tilt Holdings	TLLTF	9,653,000	-2,289,000	11,942,000
MedMen	MMNFF	-80,973,925	59,779,519	-140,753,444
Cansortium	CNTMF	8,088,000	7,433,000	655,000
Red White & Bloom	RWBYF	-34,682,774	2,404,469	-37,087,243
C21 Investments	CXXIF	9,923,725	-336,367	10,260,092
Next Green Wave	NXGWF	3,052,468	0	3,052,468
Stem Holdings	STMH	-5,028,000	0	-5,028,000
Harborside	HBORF	-1,745,544	3,760,496	-5,506,040
Medicine Man	SHWZ	-9,799,690	0	-9,799,690
Lowell Farms	LOWLF	-7,751,000	0	-7,751,000
Slang Worldwide	SLGWF	-11,859,180	0	-11,859,180
Vibe Growth	VBSCF	724,343	1,432,560	-708,217
Hollister Bio	HSTRF	-254,529	777,000	-1,031,529
Body & Mind	BMMJ	-2,310,164	1,370,121	-3,680,285
iAnthus Capital	ITHUF	-13,074,000	22,302,000	-35,376,000
Plus Products	PLPRF	-1,917,882	0	-1,917,882

The last column in Exhibit 2.8 labeled "Free Cash Flow" is designed to overcome the nonpayment of taxes problem associated with the net cash provided by operations figure. The free cash flows of all 35 cannabis companies totaled a negative $238.7 million, which differed materially from the $81.8 million in positive cash they reported as provided by their net operating activities. The difference between these measures of cash flow is striking. The most noticeable change highlighted in Exhibit 2.8 is for Curaleaf.

When Curaleaf's $57,753,000 in unpaid 2020 income taxes is taken into consideration, its $12,255,000 in reported cash provided from operations evaporates and its free cash flow becomes a negative $45,398,000. The amount of income taxes Curaleaf incurred but failed to pay in 2020 was exceeded only by MedMen.

As of December 31, 2020 MedMen was showing it had current income taxes payable of $86.3 million and Curaleaf was showing it had current income taxes payable of $79.6 million. Other cannabis companies showing large amounts of past due income taxes included Cresco $49.4 million, Verano $47.1 million, Terrascend $27.2 million, and Ayr Wellness $21.6 million.

As noted earlier in Exhibit 2.2, at the end of 2020 the amounts of income taxes payable by Curaleaf and MedMen exceeded the amount of cash they showed on their balance sheets. Chalice Brands, Cansortium, Red White & Bloom, and Body & Mind also had more income taxes payable on their balance sheets than cash.

Two of the 12 companies that reported positive operating cash flow, Curaleaf and Vibe Growth, showed negative free cash flow once their failure to pay current income taxes incurred in 2020 was considered. On the other hand, Planet 13 was able to go from a negative cash flow amount of $914,965 to a positive free cash flow of $4,879,989.

Interestingly, five companies actually paid more income taxes in 2020 than they incurred. Those five were Columbia Care, Item 9 Labs, Planet 13, Tilt Holdings, and Trulieve. As a result these five companies were able to report better free cash flow amounts than what they showed as their net operating cash.

Exhibit 2.8 shows that only 11 (31.4%) of the 35 cannabis companies were able to generate positive free cash flow in 2020. The negative free cash flow problem has been a consistent characteristic of the cannabis sector since companies started to emerge in Canada. It has been cavalierly dismissed by stakeholders as typical of early-stage companies. That excuse is becoming far less acceptable to investors.

The need for cash by cannabis companies is persistent and somewhat surprising since it is at the moment a cash business. Cannabis companies are not burdened by huge accounts receivable or bad debt expenses like so many other businesses. They also do not have major advertising expenditures, since they are burdened with onerous marketing restrictions. Of course, cannabis companies do face the cruelty of IRC Section 280E and its impact is material; however, that alone, as illustrated by Exhibit 2.8, is not a sufficient explanation for the apparent unquenchable need for cash by cannabis companies.

Belatedly, accountants are recognizing the enormity of the free cash flow problem at cannabis companies. In acts of seeming self-preservation, accountant opinion letters accompanying audited reports are increasingly including statements questioning the ability of cannabis companies to survive. Here are a few statements copied from opinion letters that accompanied the 2020 audited annual reports of companies discussed in this book.

Auditor Opinion #1

"We draw attention to Note 1 to the financial statements, which describes matters and conditions that indicate the existence of a material uncertainty that may cast significant doubt about the Company's ability to continue as a going concern. Our opinion is not modified in respect of this matter.

Note 1:

Going concern assumption These consolidated financial statements have been prepared in accordance with International Financial Reporting Standards with the assumption that the Company will be able to realize its assets and discharge its liabilities in the normal course of business. The Company's continuing operations are dependent upon its ability to raise capital and generate cash flows from operations… Although the Company achieved profitability in the latter part of 2020, it has yet to demonstrate that it can maintain profitability on a sustained basis. These circumstances indicate the existence of material uncertainty that casts significant doubt as to the Company's ability to meet its business plans and its obligations as they become due, and accordingly, the appropriateness of the use of the accounting principles applicable to a going concern.

The consolidated financial statements have been prepared on a going concern basis that assumes the Company will be able to continue to realize its assets and discharge its liabilities in the normal course of business in the foreseeable future and does not reflect the adjustments to assets and liabilities that would be necessary if it were unable to obtain adequate financing. Such adjustments could be material. If the Company is unable to raise funds and generate cash flows from operations, it may not be able to continue as a going concern."

Auditor Opinion #2

"Material Uncertainty Related to Going Concern

We draw attention to Note 1 of the consolidated financial statements, which indicates that the Company had a net loss during the year ended December 31, 2020 and, as of that date, had an accumulated deficit. As stated in Note 1, these events or conditions, along with other matters as set forth in Note 1, indicate that a material uncertainty exists that may cast significant doubt on the Company's ability to continue as a going concern. Our opinion is not modified in respect of this matter.

Note 1:

... To date, the Company has been successful in obtaining enough funding for operating and capital requirements primarily through equity and debt financings. The ability of the Company to continue as a going concern is dependent upon its ability to achieve profitable operations and renegotiate existing financings. While the Company has been effective in raising financing in the past, there is no assurance that it will be able to successfully obtain additional financing as needed."

Auditor Opinion #3

"Explanatory Paragraph - Going Concern

The accompanying consolidated financial statements have been prepared assuming that the Company will continue as a going concern. As more fully described in Note 2, the Company has a significant working capital deficiency, has incurred significant losses and needs to raise additional funds to meet its obligations and sustain its operations. These conditions raise substantial doubt about the Company's ability to continue as a going concern. Management's plans in regard to these matters are also described in Note 2. The consolidated financial statements do not include any adjustments that might result from the outcome of this uncertainty.

Note 2:

Going Concern

These consolidated financial statements have been prepared under the assumption that the Company will be able to continue its operations and will be able to realize its assets and discharge its liabilities in the normal course of business in the foreseeable future. … material circumstances cast substantial doubt on the Company's ability to continue as a going concern for a period at least twelve months from the date of this report and ultimately on the appropriateness of the use of the accounting principles applicable to a going concern."

The above auditor comments should not be taken lightly. For them to finally realize and cite the cash flow problems of cannabis companies is a major step in the right direction. The negative free cash flow problem has infected cannabis company operations and no one has been able to pinpoint the root cause or the solution.

It is possible that the current lack of cash flow and profits is a function of inept leadership by promoters' primarily interested making a quick fortune. The people who started a majority of the cannabis companies were adept at organizing companies and taking them public in IPOs guaranteed to make themselves wealthy. They understood the system and took advantage of it. Some organizers even stuck around and tried to run the cannabis companies they created, while others became serial organizers of publicly held cannabis companies. The serial organizers realized it was easier to create a fortune out of thin air than it was to operate a complex business that required knowledge of agriculture, manufacturing, packaging, marketing, public relations, accounting, et cetera.

A majority of the people now running the cannabis companies are the organizers of these companies. They do not have the necessary knowledge and experience to run the companies nor do they have enough experience in the business to hire the right people. Unfortunately, many of today's cannabis company CEOs view themselves as talented but are in fact incompetent.

The first step in solving a problem is to recognize you have a problem. The second step is to define the problem. The third step is to measure the extent of the problem. The fourth step is to manage the problem. Occasionally, a problem actually gets solved. Unfortunately, a majority of cannabis companies do not believe they have a problem.

Non-GAAP and Non-IFRS Measures

The lack of profits and cash flow in financial statements prepared using GAAP and IFRS accounting encouraged cannabis company CEOs along with their investment bankers and accountants to create a more favorable measure of performance. With that in mind, they designed a measure they strongly suggest is the best way to gauge cannabis company performance and named it Adjusted EBITDA.

Truth be told, Adjusted EBITDA is a ruse artfully crafted to separate investors from their money while feeding the egos and wallets of cannabis company CEOs. It was first introduced by the five large Canadian LPs in press releases that accompanied their quarterly earnings reports and it was accented in the conference calls and included in the Management Discussion and Analysis (MD&A) companies filed with SEDAR. Adjusted EBITDA was designed to put a positive spin on gruesome financial statements prepared using GAAP and IFRS accounting.

It is doubtful that any other industry in history has been as successful as the cannabis industry in persuading investors that profits and cash flow are not good measures of performance. Adjusted EBITDA myopia is cancerous to cannabis company shareholders, masks deep-rooted problems, and misleads investors.

History of EBITDA

EBITDA is defined as net income before interest, taxes, depreciation, and amortization. Adherents of EBITDA foster the impression that it has been the most used measure of profits and cash flow for millennia. The fact is EBITDA was invented by John Malone, a billionaire investor, as a way to entice lenders and investors to fund his rollup of cable systems in the 1970s.

Malone's preaching came before the introduction of computers. In that pre-computer era lenders were less able to measure the capacity of a company to pay and they tended to focus on character and collateral of the borrower.

Lenders who did concern themselves with a borrower's capacity to repay relied heavily on reported net income after taxes (NIAT) plus depreciation. In the early 1970s lenders actually thought NIAT + depreciation was cash flow. With such an unsophisticated measure of repayment ability, it is not surprising that Malone was able to persuade lenders that EBITDA was a superior measure of a company's earnings and cash flow.

The affection for EBITDA was evident in the dot.com era of the late 1990s when numerous technology companies went public even though they had large losses. These companies all followed Malone's playbook and convinced investors to ignore those losses and focus on riches that awaited them in the future. Unfortunately, only a few were able to survive the dot.com bust when money available to companies dried up in 2020.

Warren Buffet and his longtime partner, Charlie Munger have consistently criticized the use of EBITDA. Buffet has said "people and companies who talk about EBITDA are either trying to con you or con themselves or both. A substantial number of frauds talk about EBITDA. If you divide all the people in the world who talk about EBITDA into two groups: those who talk about EBITDA and those who do not. There are more frauds in the EBITDA group by a very substantial margin. EBITDA is utter nonsense. It is not cash flow or a good parameter to value a business. We will not buy into a company or a stock where people are talking about EBITDA. It's in the interests of Wall Street to talk about EBITDA, because it results in higher borrowing power, higher valuation, and higher investment fees. Furthermore, EBITDA is very misleading and can be used in very pernicious ways. If a company knows you are looking at EBITDA officials can arrange things to make the company look better."

Charlie Munger has said EBITDA is ridiculous and CEOs who use it are intellectually dishonest. In a terse famous statement, he said EBITDA is "bullshit."

Buffet is especially critical of the fact that EBITDA adds back depreciation, because it is a non-cash expense. He asserts that is absurd because depreciation is actually the worst kind of expense, since it represents an expense you already paid when you made the capital expenditure to which the depreciation relates.

To him, depreciation is like reverse float, since you lay out money before you get to expense it. Furthermore, he says yearly capital expenditures at Berkshire, like most other companies, generally exceed depreciation charges.

Exhibit 2.9 shows the depreciation expense and purchases of plant and equipment (CAPEX) for 35 vertically integrated companies for Q1 of 2021. CAPEX is divided by depreciation to reveal the extent to which CAPEX exceeds depreciation. The data presented in Exhibit 2.9 strongly suggests Buffet's statement that CAPEX generally exceeds depreciation also applies to U.S cannabis companies.

Exhibit 2.9
CAPEX Relative to Depreciation: 2020
(USD in thousands)

Company	Symbol	Depreciation	CAPEX	Ratio of CAPEX to Depreciation
Curaleaf	CURLF	18,538	126,273	6.8
Green Thumb	GTBIF	15,076	59,797	4.0
Trulieve	TCNNF	26,905	189,858	7.1
Cresco Labs	CRLBF	16,287	7,827	0.5
Terrascend	TRSSF	6,461	45,825	7.1
Columbia Care	CCHWF	14,891	42,885	2.9
Harvest Health	HRVSF	12,626	26,863	2.1
Chalice Brands Ltd	CHALF	1,245	169	0.1
Planet 13	PLNHF	3,641	4,481	1.2
Ayr Wellness	AYRWF	4,732	14,368	3.0
Ascend Wellness	AAWH	5,030	46,093	9.2
Jushi Holdings	JUSHF	2,889	21,706	7.5
4Front Ventures	FFNTF	2,925	13,875	4.7
Acreage Holdings	ACRHF	4,049	15,477	3.8
Goodness Holdings	GDNSF	413	8,449	20.5
Item 9 Labs	INLB	129	499	3.9
Gage Growth Corp	GAEGF	1,066	9,844	9.2
MariMed	MRMD	1,792	4,688	2.6
Tilt Holdings	TLLTF	4,160	1,908	0.5
MedMen	MMNFF	18,331	1,490	0.1
Cansortium	CNTMF	3,989	5,192	1.3
Red White & Bloom	RWBYF	4,430	-108	NM
C21 Investments	CXXIF	631	228	0.4
Next Green Wave	NXGWF	889	327	0.4
Stem Holdings	STMH	2,000	5,799	2.9
Harborside	HBORF	2,474	755	0.3
Medicine Man	SHWZ	477	769	1.6
Lowell Farms	LOWLF	3,848	6,850	1.8
Slang Worldwide	SLGWF	536	5,004	9.3
Vibe Growth	VBSCF	461	530	1.1
Hollister Bio	HSTRF	1,208	398	0.3
Body & Mind	BMMJ	1,189	872	0.7
iAnthus Capital	ITHUF	10,493	13,435	1.3
Plus Products	PLPRF	101	-233	NM

Property, plant and equipment are shown on balance sheets at cost less accumulated depreciation. Depreciation is recognized as an expense on a company income statement and the amount of depreciation taken annually is based on the expected useful life of an asset. Land is not depreciated. Typically, buildings and improvements are expensed over 7 to 40 years, furniture and equipment over 3 to 10 years, and vehicles over 3 to 5 years.

Twenty-eight (28) or 80% of the 35 cannabis companies shown in Exhibit 2.9 spent more on CAPEX in Q1 2021 than they expensed in depreciation during that quarter. Most had CAPEX much greater than their depreciation. For example, 4Front Ventures CAPEX was 15.5x its depreciation expense; Item 9 Labs CAPEX was 11.5x, Ayr Wellness CAPEX was

10.3x, Trulieve CAPEX was 9.5x, and Verano Holdings CAPEX was 8.7x its depreciation.

The data on CAPEX relative to depreciation presented in Exhibit 2.9 show EBITDA is not a great proxy for cash flow at cannabis companies. People who claim it is a good measure of cash flow need to re-examine their stance on that issue. In truth, EBITDA is a seriously flawed measure of cash generation and this illustrated example of current expenditures on plant and equipment (CAPEX) relative to depreciation is just a small sample of its shortcomings.

Evolution of Adjusted EBITDA

The affinity of cannabis companies for EBITDA was first established by the big five Canadian companies. It seemed that every earnings release and conference call by one of them featured a prognostication about positive EBITDA developments. It was natural that U.S. companies would follow the Canadian companies. After all, the lawyers, accountants, and investment bankers who catered to the Canadian companies were the same ones who catered to the U.S. cannabis companies.

The U.S. companies have taken EBITDA to levels that would likely make John Malone smile and Warren Buffet cringe. As shown earlier in this chapter, profits and free cash flow have been almost nonexistent for fully integrated U.S. cannabis companies.

The CEOs and investment bankers had to come up with something that would put a positive spin on otherwise horrible results. To fill that need vertically integrated U.S. cannabis companies created "Adjusted EBITDA," which is not approved under either GAAP or IFRS rules.

The following is a descriptive excerpt of Adjusted EBITDA from Footnote 3 of a May 10, 2021 Trulieve press release that announced the signing of a definitive agreement to acquire Harvest Health. In the body of that release Trulieve stated the combined company was expected to have Adjusted EBITDA of $461 million in 2021. That amount was defined in Footnote 3 of the release as follows:

> "This non-GAAP financial measure is based on the analysis of non-GAAP financial measures of various financial analysts, each of whom may not be calculating such financial measure in the same manner as each other or Trulieve or Harvest. This information should be considered as supplemental in nature and not as a substitute for, or superior to, any measure of performance prepared in accordance with GAAP. Our management teams use Adjusted EBITDA to evaluate our operating performance and trends and make planning decisions. Our management teams believe Adjusted EBITDA helps identify underlying trends in our business that could otherwise be masked by the effect of the items that we exclude. Accordingly, we believe that Adjusted EBITDA provides useful information to investors and others in understanding and evaluating our operating results, enhancing the overall

understanding of our past performance and future prospects of the combined company, and allowing for greater transparency with respect to key financial metrics used by our management teams in its financial and operational decision-making."

This statement by Trulieve really understates the importance its management places on Adjusted EBITDA. For example, recent acquisitions in Pennsylvania have included additional consideration payable to the sellers based on Adjusted EBITDA.

Further evidence of the singular focus by Trulieve on Adjusted EBITDA is visible in Exhibit 2.10, which shows a quarterly comparison of its net income after taxes (NIAT), free cash flow, and Adjusted EBITDA. Exhibit 2.10 reveals huge divergences between these three measures of company performance, inconsistency in NIAT and Cash Flow from quarter to quarter, and a pattern of consistent growth in Adjusted EBITDA.

Sequentially (QOQ), Trulieve NIAT declined in six out of 12 quarters. including four consecutive quarters beginning with the fourth quarter of 2019. On a year-over-year (YOY) basis Trulieve earned significantly less in every quarter in 2020 than it did in 2019 and its quarterly earnings peaked in Q3 2019 at NIAT of $60.3 million.

It is especially discomforting that as Tulieve NIAT was plummeting in 2020, its CAPEX exploded to $189.9 million from $45.4 million in 2019. Trulieve shareholders need to start seeing the benefits of that CAPEX soon in the form of higher earnings and free cash flow per share.

Without question much of the variability in NIAT was attributable to IFRS accounting and the impact of biologicals. Column 4 in Exhibit 2.10 shows the net effect of the unrealized gains on the growth of biological assets and the realized fair value amounts included in inventory sold on total revenue. The volatility of those IFRS revenue items certainly caused the observed volatility in Trulieve NIAT by artificially inflating revenue in 2019 and depressing it in 2020.

The induced volatility in NIAT is one of the primary reasons Trulieve switched to GAAP accounting, which it did with at the end of 2020. Its 2020 annual report was its first official filing using GAAP.

The switch from IFRS to GAAP ironed out all the originally reported quarterly differences shown in Exhibit 2.10. For example, the quarterly numbers reported show that Trulieve NIAT was down $107 million or 81% in the first nine months of 2020 versus the first nine months of 2019 based on the IFRS accounting and likely to report a major decline in NIAT for the year. Fortunately, the switch to GAAP prevented that from happening, since GAAP wiped away the impact of biologicals. By so doing, Trulieve was able to report is NIAT in 2020 rose by 18.7%.

Exhibit 2.10
Trulieve Performance Measures: 2018-2021
(USD in thousands)

Fiscal Quarter	NIAT	Free Cash Flow	Adjusted EBITDA	Biologicals Impact
Q1 2018	6,863	1,375	6,128	5,212
Q2 2018	7,883	6,808	11,908	3,020
Q3 2018	17,502	9,002	16,630	15,770
Q4 2018	10,720	2,149	15,248	12,939
Q1 2019	14,702	2,449	18,967	10,223
Q2 2019	57,529	9,669	31,616	66,230
Q3 2019	60,271	10,762	36,938	66,120
Q4 2019	45,530	3,453	45,020	57,354
Q1 2020	13,999	6,146	49,427	-4,420
Q2 2020	6,561	28,855	60,535	-16,796
Q3 2020	4,742	36,880	67,500	-16,787
Q4 2020	37,697	34,128	73,490	NA
Q1 2021	30,078	23,853	90,797	NA

Frankly, it is more than somewhat sacrilegious to criticize Trulieve and its volatile NIAT and free cash flow given the fact that it is the only cannabis company that has consistently produced after tax profits and positive net operating cash flow. Its shareholders surely did not complain about the poor earnings reported during the first three quarters of 2020, since its stock rose 267% from $11.84 to $31.62 in 2020. It deserves criticism, however, because its stature allows it to establish NIAT and free cash flow as the valuation metrics by which all cannabis companies should be measured. Instead, it has championed the use of Adjusted EBITDA and that is inexcusable.

Calculation of Adjusted EBITDA by Cannabis Companies

Regulatory filings were examined to identify the items that went into the calculation of Adjusted EBITDA by vertically integrated cannabis companies. That examination identified 44 different items used by various cannabis companies to calculate their Adjusted EBITDA. More probably exist but were not disclosed in the filings and more are probably being concocted at this moment.

These 44 items are presented alphabetically in Exhibit 2.11 where they could have been labeled ingredients, since each cannabis company seems to pride itself on its own recipe for calculating its version. Ingredients, recipe, and cooking the books do not seem inappropriate when one considers the insidious ways cannabis companies use Adjusted EBITDA.

As company filings were examined and additional adjustment items continued to be identified, a feeling emerged that raised serious questions about the integrity of financial reports within the publicly held cannabis industry and the length to which companies would go to paint a glowing picture. The extensive list of items and the small amounts per item conveyed the impression that the company accountants were scraping the bottom of the barrel in an all out effort to inflate results. When one reads the statements that accompany an Adjusted EBITDA report; such as, these numbers have not been approved by GAAP or IFRS and they cannot be compared with other companies then an element of fear emerges.

Cannabis company CEOs know they are skating on thin ice when they start touting their favored financial metrics. Accordingly, here is a typical disclosure statement made by cannabis companies and designed by lawyers to offer protection against lawsuits by unhappy shareholders.

The fact that cannabis company CEOs have been able to brandish Adjusted EBITDA may in fact be attributable to the financial naïveté of the typical cannabis stock investor. Institutional investors have generally been absent from the publicly held cannabis sector, so they have not been there to challenge cannabis company CEOs and CFOs. It will be surprising if cannabis company executives are allowed to use their latest, greatest performance measure when professional money managers appear on the scene. Knowledgeable investors will not allow cannabis company CEOs, CFOs, and investor relations heads to continue their financial charade.

The following is a statement excerpted from the Ayr Wellness Management Discussion and Analysis (MD&A) filed with SEDAR on March 10, 2021. Identical or nearly identical statements can be found in every cannabis company MD&A.

Exhibit 2.11
Cannabis Adjusted EBITDA Items

Net Income (Loss) Before Taxes
- Interest
- Income Tax
- Depreciation
- Amortization

EBITDA
- Realized fair value amounts included in inventory sold
- Unrealized fair value gain on growth of biological assets

EBITDA after Adjusting for Difference in IFRS/GAAP Treatment of Biologicals
- Acquisition costs
- Amortization of loan discount on debt to equity conversion
- Bad debt expense
- Capital raise related expenses
- Costs to acquire real estate
- Costs associated with IFRS to GAAP conversion
- Costs to obtain licenses and permits
- Covid-19 related expenses
- Cultivation costs expenses
- Deal related expenses
- Depreciation included in cost of goods sold
- De-SPAC costs
- Discontinued operations
- Earnout liability accrual
- Expansion costs
- Expected credit losses on financial assets and related charges
- Fair value mark-up for acquired inventory
- Foreign currency gain (loss)
- Impairment of goodwill
- Impairment of intangible assets
- Impairment of property, plant and equipment
- Indemnification costs
- Interest expense in cost of goods sold
- Inventory Step-up, fair value
- Lease Restructuring Costs
- Legal settlement
- Listing fee expense
- Loss on investments in associates
- Loss on lease termination
- Loss on remeasurement of assets held for sale
- Marketing infrastructure improvements
- Net change in fair value of warrants and derivative liabilities
- Non-cash writedowns of inventory
- Non-recurring expenses
- Pre-acquisition expense
- Pre-opening expansion expenses
- Realized gain (loss) on investments
- Rebranding costs
- Relaunch costs
- Relief of fair value of inventory upon acquisition
- Rent Adjustment
- Restructuring costs
- Revaluation of contingencies
- Sales and marketing expense
- Severance costs
- Share based compensation
- Start-up costs
- Transaction costs
- Unrealized gain on note receivable
- Unrealized loss on investments

"**Definition and Reconciliation of Non-IFRS Measures**

The Corporation reports certain non-IFRS measures that are used to evaluate the performance of such businesses and the performance of their respective segments, as well as to manage their capital structure. As non-IFRS measures generally do not have a standardized meaning, they may not be comparable to similar measures presented by other issuers. Securities regulations require such measures to be clearly defined and reconciled with their most directly comparable IFRS measure. The Corporation references non-IFRS measures including cannabis industry metrics, in this document and elsewhere. These measures are not recognized measures under IFRS and do not have a standardized meaning prescribed by IFRS and are therefore unlikely to be comparable to similar measures presented by other companies. Rather, these are provided as additional information to complement those IFRS measures by providing further understanding of the results of the operations of the Corporation from management's perspective. Accordingly, these measures should not be considered in isolation, nor as a substitute for analysis of the Corporation's financial information reported under IFRS. Non-IFRS measures used to analyze the performance of the Corporation include "Adjusted EBITDA". The Corporation believes that these non-IFRS financial measures provide meaningful supplemental information regarding the Corporation's performances and may be useful to investors because they allow for greater transparency with respect to key metrics used by management in its financial and operational decision-making. These financial measures are intended to provide investors with supplemental measures of the Corporation's operating performances and thus highlight trends in the Corporation's core businesses that may not otherwise be apparent when solely relying on the IFRS measures."

The IFRS Foundation is a not-for-profit, public interest organization established to develop a single set of high-quality, understandable, enforceable and globally accepted accounting standards. IFRS Standards are set by the IFRS Foundation's standard-setting body, the International Accounting Standards Board. IFRS Standards are developed to bring transparency, accountability and efficiency to financial markets around the world. Publicly accountable companies (those listed on public stock exchanges) and financial institutions are legally required to publish their financial reports in accordance with agreed accounting standards.

Most cannabis companies were formed in Canada and listed on Canadian stock exchanges and they use IFRS accounting. All companies registered with the SEC use GAAP standards which are promulgated by the Financial Accounting Standards Board FASB). Like IFRS, GAAP aims to promote transparency and consistency.

With such altruistic purposes, why is it that IFRS and GAAP will not allow the use of Adjusted EBITDA? What do they know that you do not know? Is it possible that they see concerted attempts by company executives to mislead investors by creating financial metrics that are easily manipulated to the benefit of insiders?

The accounting standards established by GAAP and IFRS are certainly not perfect, but they make sure we drive on the correct side of the road to prevent chaos. The introduction of Adjusted EBITDA, Adjusted EBITDA margin, adjusted sales, and numerous new metrics popping up in cannabis company financial presentations create an unacceptable degree of financial opaqueness at a time when investors are demanding transparency.

Main Ingredients of Adjusted EBITDA

There is a growing chorus of astute cannabis stock investors who are highly critical of Adjusted EBITDA. Their dislike centers on a belief this is a deceitful measure artfully designed by cannabis company CEOs, company insiders, accountants, and investment bankers who want to line their pockets with money ripped off from unsuspecting investors. Critics believe Adjusted EBITDA obscures high levels of debt, huge tax bills, meager or nonexistent earnings, escalating acquisition expenses, and large amounts of non-cash compensation to insiders.

Exhibit 2.12 sheds light on this criticism by showing interest, taxes, and share-based compensation as percentages of Adjusted EBITDA for 35 U.S. cannabis companies. Fifteen of the 35 companies in Exhibit 2.12 reported negative Adjusted EBITDA for fiscal 2020. Obviously, the reported Adjusted EBITDA of every company would have been reduced if back out interest, taxes, or share-based compensation from their calculation.

Interest

Exhibit 2.12 shows five companies where interest accounted for more than 100% of their Adjusted EBITDA. If interest alone was not added back to net income after taxes, Harvest Health, 4Front Ventures, Cansortium, Red White & Bloom, and Harborside company would have reported negative Adjusted EBITDA instead of the positive numbers they reported.

For example, Harvest Health reported a net loss after taxes of $59.6 million. To arrive at its reported Adjusted EBITDA it chose to add back or deduct the impact of the following 13 items: net interest including financing costs ($39.0 million), income taxes ($3.7 million), amortization and depreciation ($11.3), impairments ($0.7 million), asset sales

($11.8 million), fair value liability adjustment ($10.1 million), other expenses ($17.2 million), foreign currency gain $0.1 million), share-based compensation ($22.5 million), asset recovery ($0.7 million), discontinued operations ($1.3 million), expansion expenses ($12.7 million), and other special charges ($1.8 million). Once those items were added back the $59.6 million loss became an Adjusted EBITDA of $15.3 million.

Even John Scarne, the famous "card sharp" would be impressed by how cleverly a $59.6 million dollar loss can be turned into something purported to be wonderful!

Exhibit 2.12				
Interest, Taxes, Share-Based Compensation				
Expressed as Percentages of Adjusted EBITDA for 2020				
Company	Symbol	Interest	Taxes	Share-based Compensation
Curaleaf	CURLF	33.2%	57.9%	21.4%
Green Thumb	GTBIF	10.4%	46.7%	10.8%
Trulieve	TCNNF	8.1%	37.6%	1.1%
Verano Holdings	VRNOF	4.1%	45.2%	0.0%
Cresco Labs	CRLBF	34.0%	37.7%	15.9%
Terrascend	TRSSF	6.4%	94.6%	27.6%
Columbia Care	CCHWF	-334.2%	88.6%	-699.3%
Harvest Health	HRVSF	254.3%	23.8%	146.6%
Chalice Brands Ltd	CHALF	-168.8%	-168.8%	-47.2%
Planet 13	PLNHF	20.2%	20.2%	28.2%
Ayr Wellness	AYRWF	7.3%	7.3%	55.4%
Ascend Wellness	AAWH	42.1%	60.7%	2.2%
Jushi Holdings	JUSHF	-722.6%	-397.6%	-278.7%
4Front Ventures	FFNTF	268.4%	262.9%	90.2%
Acreage Holdings	ACRHF	-53.7%	58.4%	-312.0%
Goodness Holdings	GDNSF	-97.4%	-168.0%	-244.3%
Item 9 Labs	INLB	-689.5%	8.6%	-74.5%
Gage Growth Corp	GAEGF	-19.1%	-39.6%	-140.7%
MariMed	MRMD	54.9%	11.6%	5.6%
Tilt Holdings	TLLTF	61.1%	-29.8%	24.8%
MedMen	MMNFF	-32.7%	35.2%	-4.6%
Cansortium	CNTMF	133.7%	61.6%	55.8%
Red White & Bloom	RWBYF	175.7%	-80.0%	101.4%
C21 Investments	CXXIF	42.3%	24.2%	5.1%
Next Green Wave	NXGWF	33.5%	27.1%	11.4%
Stem Holdings	STMH	-33.6%	0.0%	-28.6%
Harborside	HBORF	662.0%	859.9%	148.9%
Medicine Man	SHWZ	-0.2%	5.0%	-45.7%
Lowell Farms	LOWLF	-39.3%	-2.6%	-26.0%
Slang Worldwide	SLGWF	-4.5%	47.7%	-170.4%
Vibe Growth	VBSCF	5.0%	57.1%	4.5%
Hollister Bio	HSTRF	-11.9%	-71.4%	-62.4%
Body & Mind	BMMJ	0.1%	-173.8%	30.3%
iAnthus Capital	ITHUF	-61.9%	-59.7%	0.0%
Plus Products	PLPRF	-30.7%	38.5%	-35.1%

If interest alone of $39.0 million is backed out Harvest's reported EBITDA of $15.3 million would drop to a negative $23.6 million. The same reversals from positive Adjusted EBITDA to negative would also apply to 4Front Ventures, Cansortium, Red White & Bloom, and Harborside.

Harborside reported Adjusted EBITDA of $711,000, but without adding its interest of $4.708 million to its net income after taxes it would have had an Adjusted EBITDA of a negative $3.997 million.

Interest expense also had significant impact on the Adjusted EBITDA reported by Jushi Holdings, Item 9 Labs, Columbia Care, and Chalice Brands. Each of those companies reported negative Adjusted EBITDA, but without adding back their interest expense their negative amounts would have been magnified several times. As an example, Jushi Holdings reported negative Adjusted EBITDA of $2.616 million would have been a negative $21.518 million if it had not added back the interest of $18.902 million.

Interest expense represented an average of 45.9% of the total Adjusted EBITDA reported by the 35 companies in Exhibit 2.12. It ranged from a high of 722.6% for Jushi Holdings to a low of 0.1% for Body & Mind.

Taxes

Taxes are shown in Exhibit 2.12 as a percentage of Adjusted EBITDA to gauge the importance of taxes in calculating that measure. Columbia Care, Acreage Holdings, Item 9 Labs, Tilt Holdings, MedMen, Red White & Bloom, Slang Worldwide, Body & Mind, and Plus Products all reported tax refunds in 2020.

Positive Adjusted EBITDA reported by 4Front Ventures and Harborside would have been negative if they had not added taxes in their tabulation of Adjusted EBITDA. 4Front's $5.88 million would have been a negative $9.581 million, while Harborside's $711,000 would have been a negative $5.404 million.

Taxes represented an average of 53.6% of the total Adjusted EBITDA reported by the 35 companies in Exhibit 2.12. Taxes ranged from a high of 859.9 percent of Adjusted EBITDA at Harborside to a low of 0 at Stem Holdings, which reported no tax liability or refund.

When cannabis companies are concocting their special versions of Adjusted EBITDA it does not seem to matter to them if the taxes are current taxes or deferred taxes. It also does not seem to matter if the current taxes are paid or not. The most import objective of cannabis companies is to make sure their Adjusted EBITDA is bigger than its peers and if that requires some prestidigitation well - so be it!

Share-Based Compensation

Share-based compensation is rising dramatically at cannabis companies after executives have watched SPAC sponsors enrich themselves without the slightest sense guilt. Exhibit 2.12 shows share-based compensation as a percentage of Adjusted EBITDA for 35 cannabis companies. Share-based compensation in 2020 totaled $341.3 million at these companies and ranged from a high of $92.1 million at Acreage Holdings to a low of $11,350 at iAnthus. The average of all companies, excluding Verano, was $10.0 million and 40.2% of Adjusted EBITDA.

Share-based compensation seemed to be especially noteworthy at Acreage Holdings where insiders awarded themselves $92.1 million in share-based compensation in 2020 even though it had a loss of $360.1 million. If that compensation was not added, Acreage would have reported negative Adjusted EBITDA of $121.571 million instead of its negative $29.507 million.

Acreage Holdings has been a troubled U.S. MSO almost since its birth at the hands of Wall Street financiers who were touted as being able to create great wealth because of their financial wizardry. Acreage is now being criticized by other Wall Street wizards who claim those guys just didn't have the right stuff.

The new financial alchemists have backgrounds in designing exotic derivatives, selling stocks and bonds, and doing and road shows to promote the latest greatest investment idea. They purport to have magic dashboards that allow them to dial up numbers that will be generated by businesses they know close to nothing about. They have little or no knowledge about the complexities of operating a vertically integrated agricultural business, but the one thing they all share is an abundance of chutzpah. Cannabis investors need to avoid these charlatans.

Ayr Wellness executives showed no shame by awarding themselves $31,157,000 in share-based compensation in a year it reported a net loss after taxes of $176.333 million. They are among the leading advocates of Adjusted EBITDA and it is easy to see why. After all, the $31.157 million share-based compensation they awarded themselves amounted to only 55.4% of their concocted Adjusted EBITDA. So, what could be wrong with that?

A similar situation existed at Columbia Care where insiders awarded themselves $28.937 million in share-based compensation even though it had a net loss of $110.776 million. If share-based compensation was not added, Columbia Care would have reported a negative Adjusted EBITDA of $33.075 instead of a negative $4.138 million.

It goes without saying that insiders awarding themselves outsized share-based compensation when a company is losing money and burning cash reeks! The fact that it is added back in calculating Adjusted EBITDA helps explain why CEOs like to focus investor attention away from earnings and free cash flow and onto Adjusted EBITDA.

It should be noted that there were a few, but very few, publicly held cannabis companies where the insiders did not totally cover themselves in share-based compensation shame in 2020. The largest of those companies was Trulieve which reported $2.8 million in share-based compensation amounting to only 4.4% of its net income and 1.1% of its Adjusted EBITDA. Others that deserve mention for their lack of insider greed in 2020 are Ascend Wellness, MariMed, C21 Investments, and Vibe Growth.

Investors clearly need to take a careful look at the share-based compensation that cannabis company insiders award themselves. The amounts awarded in 2020 are alarming when expressed as percentages of income. It is a special insult when the amount of share-based compensation is added back to inflate EBITDA, which is then used by insiders to reward themselves with more share-based compensation.

Adjusted EBITDA Margin

Cannabis company CEOs have recently elevated their ultimate measure of performance, Adjusted EBITDA, to a whole new level by the addition of "Adjusted EBITDA Margin" and an EV/Adjusted EBITDA ratio.

Adjusted EBITDA profit margin is defined as Adjusted EBITDA divided by net revenue. Its proponents suggest it is a far better measure of cannabis company true margins than old, stone age margin measures like gross profit margin and net operating margin.

EV is enterprise value and it is defined as a company's market capitalization plus preferred equity plus debt plus minority interests minus cash and investments. EBITDA fans believe the ratio of EV to Adjusted EBIDA is the ultimate way to determine the value of a business. Advocates of the EV/EBITDA ratio generally scoff at price earnings (PE) ratios, free cash flow, book value, and other measures. Their ranks are rife with insiders, investment bankers, and other stakeholders whose lives revolve around justifying higher and higher prices for stocks that will increase their personal net worth.

The fact that Adjusted EBITDA Margin and EV/Adjusted Margin are being emphasized by cannabis company CEOs, their accountants, and investment bankers at a time when cannabis stocks have fallen by 30% is not accidental. People with vested interests will do whatever is necessary to increase their wealth.

Today's cannabis company CEOs are simply taking a page out of John Malone's playbook he used to raise cash in the 1970s. Based on their inability to earn a profit and generate free cash flow, it is understandable they would create measures artfully crafted to lure money from unsophisticated investors who lack even rudimentary knowledge of accounting.

Summary

This chapter has endeavored to provide a methodological approach for individual investors to evaluate vertically integrated cannabis companies. It has examined balance sheets, income statements, and cash flow statements to reveal the significant information they contain that sheds light on the financial condition of numerous cannabis companies.

This chapter has shown the extreme lengths to which cannabis company executives will go to spin a tall tale of their performance. It is somewhat surprising they have not figured out how to repeal double entry bookkeeping or financial reporting altogether.

The degree of financial reporting obfuscation raises serious questions about the integrity of the people in charge of many cannabis companies. As a result, cannabis company investors must be unbelievably vigilant and somewhat skeptical about pronouncements coming out of cannabis companies.

It is clear that there is a major shortage of executive talent with the knowledge and experience necessary to successfully operate vertically integrated cannabis companies. The lack of that talent is revealed in the financial results that have been produced by most cannabis companies showing they cannot earn a profit or generate free cash flow.

The current generation of company executives is composed of promoters who cut their teeth forming companies, raising money, and taking those companies public in IPOs. They do not backgrounds in botany, horticulture, aquaculture, and numerous other agricultural sciences necessary to define, measure, and manage problems in cultivating cannabis. They also have never operated a processing facility that required products to be certified by lab technicians and outside health organizations before they were packaged. Most of them also never had to pick locations for retail establishment which they then had to design and build. Face with these and many more tasks it is not surprising many of the original recipients decided to cash out and sell their licenses for tens of millions of dollars.

If institutional investors were present in the publicly held U.S. cannabis space things would improve dramatically because they would have the power and knowledge to root out the under qualified and the ones with serious character flaws. Unfortunately, the current owners of cannabis stocks tend to be cannabis consumers with limited knowledge of company finances who are ill equipped to precipitate change.

The newness of publicly held cannabis companies precluded doing a proper time series analysis and examining several years of financial information that would show trends. The passage of time will, however, allow investors to take multiple snapshots of company financial statements to determine trends as they emerge. Accordingly, data presented in this chapter need to be updated as companies publish their financial results.

In the near future a number of the companies presented in this chapter will either be acquired or fail, while others will become dominant. Careful attention, therefore, needs to be paid to press releases and quarterly financial reports.

CHAPTER 3

PROVIDERS OF ANCILLARY PRODUCTS AND SERVICES

While a majority of vertically integrated, publicly held cannabis companies have been unable to generate a profit and free cash flow, companies providing ancillary products and services to cannabis companies have enjoyed record financial results. Observers looking at this financial dichotomy can't help but draw an analogy to the merchants who prospered by selling picks, shovels, food, and clothing and lending money to crazed prospectors during the 1840s California gold rush. Seemingly, all the merchants in that bygone era made fortunes, but very few of the prospectors did.

The providers of ancillary products and services to cannabis companies include lawyers, accountants, investment bankers, lenders, armored car services, lessors, building contractors, HVAC suppliers, hydroponics specialists, laboratories, nutrient companies, lighting companies, agronomists, IT companies, web developers, and many others. Most of these providers have customers outside of the cannabis industry and most are privately held entities.

This chapter examines only publicly held companies that provide ancillary products and services to cannabis companies. Some of these companies derive 100% of their revenue from cannabis companies and represent "pure plays." Others obtain only a small percentage of their business from cannabis companies.

These companies do not "touch the plant," therefore; they are not subject to IRC Section 280E. Accordingly, providers of products and services to cannabis companies are allowed the same tax deductions as all other corporations. In 2019, NASDAQ started allowing U.S. cannabis companies to list on its exchange so long as they are not directly involved in the cultivation, processing or sale of cannabis.

Innovative Industrial Properties, Inc.

Without question the most successful publicly held "provider" is Innovative Industrial Properties, which is headquartered in San Diego, California. It was founded in December 2016 to provide funding to licensed cannabis cultivators in medical use states. It is a self-advised corporation focused on providing funds to experienced, state-licensed medical-use operators for cultivation, processing, distribution, and retail facilities.

IIPR was incorporated in Maryland on June 15, 2016. It conducts its business through a traditional umbrella partnership real estate investment trust, or UPREIT structure, in which its properties are owned by an Operating Partnership, directly or through subsidiaries. IIPR is the sole general partner of the Operating Partnership and owns, directly or through subsidiaries, 100% of the limited partnership interests in the Operating Partnership.

In a typical IIPR transaction it buys freestanding industrial and retail properties from a state-licensed medical-use cannabis operator while agreeing to lease back the properties. Its leases are long-term triple net leases whereby the tenant pays all the expenses of the property including real estate taxes, insurance, and maintenance. Many of these transactions provide for additional funding for expansion.

IIPR targets $5 million to $30+ million sized transactions. Its lease terms range from 10-20 years. The initial rent paid by tenants is 10%-16% of the transaction amount. IIPR leases also contain escalating clauses that raise the rent payments by 3% to 4.5% every year.

REIT investors tend to be attracted to yield and there is an extremely high correlation between interest rates and REIT stocks. IIPR shareholders have benefited from the low level of interest rates. Shareholders have also benefited because IIPR established almost a monopolistic niche in an industry with an unquenchable need for external funding.

In simplest terms IIPR uses investor funds to acquire operating facilities from medical-use license holders. They are able to acquire properties on extremely favorable terms, since the borrowers have limited access to funds due to cannabis being listed as a Schedule 1 drug.

IIPR elected to be taxed as a real estate investment trust (REIT) commencing with the year ended December 31, 2017. As a REIT it must distribute at least 90% of its taxable income to shareholders.

The IIPR S-1 registration statement to go public was declared effective by the SEC on November 30, 2016. On December 1, 2016 IIPR announced an IPO of 3,350,000 shares at a price of $20 per share. An additional 502,500 share option at the IPO price was granted to and exercised by the underwriters.

It has paid quarterly dividends to shareholders since the second quarter of 2017, when it paid $0.15 per common share. The dividend has risen consistently and dramatically and for the quarter ended June 30, 2021 it paid $1.40, almost 10x its original dividend. IIPR is the only publicly held "pure cannabis company" that pays a cash dividend. Its annual dividend rate as of June 30, 2021 was 2.9%.

On June 30, 2021 IIPR closed at $191.02, which gave it a CAGR (excluding dividends) of 63.62%. Its stock price on June 30, 2021 was 9.55x its IPO price. IIPR was among the highest performing stocks for the 4 ½ year period from January 1, 2017 through June 30, 2021.

As of March 31, 2021 IIPR owned $1.1 billion in real estate properties and expected to receive at least $175 million in revenue from tenants in 2021. IIPR, therefore, has an average gross return of about 16% on its invested money and that return is expected to increase each year by about 3% from annual escalators, so in 2022 its average gross return should increase to 16.5%. Meanwhile, in May 2021 IIPR was able to issue $300 million in Senior Notes due 2026 at a 5.5% rate.

Exhibit 3.1 shows IIPR net income and cash flow provided by operations for its fiscal 2018, 2019, and 2020 years. The number of diluted shares outstanding at the end of each year along with the stock price are shown along with the resulting market capitalization, which is calculated by multiplying the number of fully diluted shares by the prevailing stock price. Exhibit 3.1 shows IIPR net income in 2020 of $65.7 million was 9.4x the $7.0 it earned in 2018. Cash flow also increased dramatically from $15.7 to $110.8 or 7.1 times. In those three years IIPR market cap grew eleven-fold from $407 million to $4.529 billion.

Exhibit 3.1
Innovative Industrial Properties Results: 2018-2020

(USD in millions)

Year	Net Income	Cash From Operations	Diluted Shares	IIPR Price	Market Cap
2018	7.0	15.7	9.8	41.62	407.9
2019	23.5	44.9	12.0	71.79	861.5
2020	65.7	110.8	25.1	180.44	4,529.0

IIPR has not been without its detractors. It was blindsided by a 36-page Grizzly Research report in April 2020 claiming that the IIPR portfolio contained low quality assets. It said IIPR had over lent to medical marijuana companies that were either insolvent or at the risk of becoming insolvent. Grizzly also asserted the portfolio was heavily concentrated with one tenant. The report was quickly refuted by IIPR executives. The downward pressure on the stock from $80 to $70 was reversed within a month and within two months IIPR was setting new high closes.

IIPR was able to achieve its impressive results because it effectively lends at 16.5%, borrows at 5.5%, and has very low expenses. It therefore has an extremely high profit margin. As long as cannabis companies are willing and able to pay such astronomical effective rates of interest and IIPR is able to obtain funds at a lower rate, IIPR will enjoy outsized net income that will be returned to shareholders in the form of dividends. If tenant defaults and or the general level of interest rates rise then the price of IIPR would come under some downward pressure.

GrowGeneration

Another corporation that has benefited greatly from being identified as a significant supplier to cannabis businesses is GrowGeneration. It is a Michigan- based indoor garden supply center that markets and distributes nutrients, growing media, advanced indoor and greenhouse lighting, environmental control systems, and accessories for hydroponic gardening of hemp, fruits, vegetables, and cannabis. It has focused increasingly on cannabis which its CEO believes offers explosive potential as more states legalize marijuana.

To capitalize on that growth, in the first quarter of 2021 GrowGeneration closed nine acquisitions and added 15 hydroponic retail location to end the quarter with a store count of 53. It now claims to be the largest chain of hydroponic garden centers in North America. Commercial Accounts are assigned a dedicated Account Manager, Customer Service Representative, and Quoting Specialist to satisfy needs from seed to harvest, including turnkey facility designs, cultivation room designs, and on-site project consultations. GrowGeneration strives to increase yields, lower production costs, and generally increase the productivity of any cultivation facility.

GrowGeneration plans to have 55 to 60 stores and to be in 15 states by the end of 2021. Its client list includes most of the large fully integrated publicly held companies in the U.S. as well as large private operators. It carries 10,000 SKUs with about 3,000 available in its stores.

Exhibit 3.2 shows some recent financial results for GrowGeneration. Its stock, which trades on the NASDAQ under the symbol GRWG, has been a top performer for the last few years. In 2019 it rose by 82% then in 2020 is went parabolic and rose tenfold from $4.10 to $40.22.

Exhibit 3.2
GrowGeneration Results: 2018-2020
(USD in millions)

Year	Net Income	Cash From Operations	Diluted Shares	End of Year GRWG Price	Market Cap
2018	-5.1	-1.5	27.9	2.25	62.8
2019	1.3	-3.3	36.9	4.10	151.3
2020	5.3	-0.2	57.2	40.22	2,300.6

In the last three years GrowGeneration has increased its net income after taxes to $5.5 million after earning $1.3 million in 2019 and losing $5.1 million in 2018. Cash provided by operations was negative in all three years, but by only $213,790.

GrowGeneration has taken advantage of the surge in its stock price by more than doubling the amount of shares it has outstanding from 27.9 million shares at the end of 2018 to 57.2 million shares at the end of 2020. Issuance of shares raised sufficient cash to fund their acquisitions while leaving them with a abundance of cash.

In the process of buying other garden supply operations, GrowGeneration increased its Goodwill from $600,000 at the end of 2017 to $8.8 million in 2018, $17.8 million in 2019, and $63.0 million at the end of 2020. The increases in goodwill and intangible assets along with negative cash provided by operations and modest profits help explain why GRWG is among the most shorted stocks.

GRWG does not pay a dividend. At mid-year 2021 it was selling at a PE Ratio above 150 based on its then trailing 12-month earnings. With such a lofty PE it is not surprising that short sellers have been attracted to GrowGeneration.

A recent calculation showed short interest was about 23% of GRWG float and it was increasing. Reddit investors might take the short interest as a buy sign, while others take it as a sell sign. Time will tell.

Scotts Miracle-Gro

Scotts Miracle Grow was perhaps the first company to gain the interest of those investors who wanted to buy companies that would benefit from growth in the cannabis industry. In anticipation of a surge in business Scotts actually established a subsidiary to concentrate of the cannabis sector.

Scotts manufactures and supplies lawn care products, and has expanded into the hydroponics supply space for **marijuana growers** with its Hawthorne Gardening subsidiary. Unlike GrowGeneration, however, Scotts is not a retailer. Another major difference is the fact that Scotts sales dwarf those of GrowGeneration.

Scotts Hawthorne subsidiary is a leading advocate of responsible legalization of marijuana. It markets Gavita, General Hydroponics, Sun System, Botanicare, Mother Earth and other brands that span every growing category including lighting, nutrients, growing environment, growing media, and hardware brands to commercial cultivators and home hobbyists.

Hawthorne subsidiary sales were up 61.4% in 2020 and amounted to $1.1 billion, representing 26.2% of Scotts total sales of $4.1 billion. Its profit amounted to $120.1 million in 2020, which was an increase of 124.5% above the 2019 profit of $53.5 million. Hawthorne 2020 net profit was 14.7% of Scotts net profit of $817.9.

SMG trades on the NYSE and ended 2018 at $57.01, 2019 at 100.94, and 2020 at 198.02. Investors in SMG did well from 2018 through 2020, but their return was well below IIPR and GRWG which were purer cannabis plays.

Jazz Pharmaceuticals

GW Pharmaceuticals would have been considered a fully integrated, publicly held cannabis company if it had remained independent. Its acquisition by Jazz Pharmaceuticals established GW Pharma as a relative small portion of Jazz. In that regard, the role cannabis may play in the future of Jazz may be similar to the impact the Hawthorne Subsidiary has on Scotts results.

In the year prior to the Jazz acquisition GW Pharma had sales of $572.2 million, while Jazz had sales of $2.4 billion. Based on these figures, GW Pharma will likely represent about 25% of Jazz total sales revenue. That percentage merits its inclusion in the group of companies presented in this chapter; however, any discussion of financials must wait until post-merger operating results are generated.

Hydrofarm Holdings

Hydrofarm is an over 40 year old horticultural products company that sells only to retailers in the U.S. and Canada. It went public in an IPO on December 14, 2020 at a price of $20 per share. It is a manufacturer and distributor of controlled environment agriculture equipment (principally hydroponics) and supplies, including high-intensity grow lights, climate control solutions, and growing media. Its stock trades on the NASDAQ under the symbol HYFM.

From 2006 through 2020Hydrofarm grew its net sales at about a 17% compound annual rate of growth (CAGR) with part of that increase attributable to growth in the cannabis sector. The company believes that a majority of the equipment and supplies it sells to customers is ultimately purchased by participants in the cannabis industry; however, it has no way to measure that since it sells only to retailers, not the end user.

Recent legalization of marijuana by several states leads Hydrofarm to believe that growth in the size of the cannabis market will have a very significant, positive impact on its business. At this point it is impossible to discern what percentage of Hydrofarm's business is attributable to cannabis. Hydrofarm says it is a large and growing portion of its business.

In 2020 Hydrofarm reported a net loss after taxes of $7.3 million on $342 million in sales. In 2019 its net loss after taxes was $40.0 million on $235.1 million in sales. As of March 31, 2021 it was showing an accumulated deficit of $149 million. On that date HYFM closed at $60.32 giving Hydrofarm a market capitalization of $2.05 billion.

Greenlane Holdings, Inc.

Greenlane is based in Boca Raton, Florida and is included among the providers because it sells cannabis accessories. It was founded in 2005 as a single-product distributor of desktop vaporizers and has evolved into a global seller of cannabis accessories and liquid nicotine products. Its revenue comes from both business-to-business (B2B) transactions, wholesale distribution to retailers, and business-to-consumer (B2C) sales. In 2020 B2B transactions accounted for 60.4% of sales, while B2C accounted for about 14.3%. More than 80% of its sales in 2020 were in the United States.

Greenlane Holdings, Inc. is a holding company formed as a Delaware corporation on May 2, 2018. It was created to complete an IPO in order to carry on the business of Greenlane Holdings, LLC, which is the Boca Raton based Operating Company formed as a Delaware corporation on September 1, 2015.

GNLN is the sole manager of the Operating Company and its principal asset is Common Units of the Operating Company. As the sole manager of the Operating Company, GNLN operates and controls all of the business and affairs of the Operating Company, and it conducts its business through the Operating Company and its subsidiaries. GNLN has a board of directors and executive officers, but no employees.

As of the end of 2020, Greenlane Holdings, Inc. had 100% of the voting power and controlled the management of the Operating Company; however, it only had a 31.6% economic interest. GNLN is designated a variable interest entity (VIE) and began consolidating the Operating Company financials with the quarter ended June 30, 2019. In so doing they itemize the amount of income (loss) as well as equity attributable to GNLN shareholders.

The GNLN corporate structure is commonly referred to as an "Up-C" structure, which is often used by partnerships and limited liability companies when they undertake an initial public offering of their business. The Up-C structure allows the members of the Operating Company to continue to realize tax benefits associated with owning interests in an entity that is treated as a partnership, or "pass-through" entity, for income tax purposes following the IPO.

One of these benefits is that future taxable income of the Operating Company that is allocated to its members will be taxed on a flow-through basis; and, therefore, will not be subject to corporate taxes at the Operating Company entity level. Additionally, because the members may redeem their Common Units for shares of GNLN Class A common stock on a one-for-one basis for cash, the Up-C structure also provides the members with potential liquidity that holders of non-publicly traded limited liability companies are not typically afforded.

The balance sheet at the end of 2020 showed GNLN shareholders had equity of $15.065. They also had an accumulated deficit of $24.848 million, which was $15.121 million larger than the deficit it reported at year end 2019 of $9.727 million. The Operating Company lost $39.8 million in 2019 and $47.7 million in 2020. GNLN reported its shareholders portion of those losses amounted to $28.8 million and $14.5 million, respectively.

For the quarter ended March 31, 2021 GNLN reported a loss attributable to its shareholders of $4.256 million compared to a loss of $4.461 for the same quarter in 2020. Its market capitalization was $91.4 million at the 2021's first quarter.

GNLN began trading on NASDAQ on April 18, 2019 and traded as high as $29 before closing at $21.10. It then began a descent reaching single digit territory by late June 2019. GNLN continued its decline reaching a closing low of $1.21 per share on March 16, 2020. A year later on March 30, 2021 GNLN closed at $4.09 on volume of 533,600 shares.

KushCo Holdings, Inc.

KushCo was founded in 2010 and is headquartered in Cypress, California. It was formerly known as Kush Bottles, Inc. It markets and sells packaging products, vaporizers, solvents, accessories, and branding solutions to customers operating in the regulated medical and adult recreational cannabis and hemp-derived cannabidiol (CBD) industries in the United States, Canada, and internationally. Its principal products include bottles, jars, bags, tubes, containers, vape cartridges, vape batteries and accessories, labels and processing supplies, solvents, natural products, stainless steel tanks, and custom branded anti-counterfeit and authentication labels. The company also offers hemp trading and retail services. The company sells products to the business-to-business market, which includes brand owners, farmers, growers, processors, producers, distributors, and licensed retailers in states with legal medical and/or adult recreational use cannabis programs and legal CBD programs through its direct sales force and e-commerce website.

In its latest fiscal year KushCo reported a net loss after taxes of $77.7 million which was about twice the previous year loss of $39.6. The loss raised its accumulated deficit to $140.7 million and it was forced to issue more shares to avoid reporting negative shareholder equity. For its fiscal 2020 KSHB also reported cash provided by operations was a negative $19.7 million.

On its first day of trading KSHB closed at $5.63. It reached a high close on February 22, 2019 of $6.38 and a low close of $0.4320 on September 23, 2020.

Greenlane Holdings and KushCo Merger

On March 31, 2021 KushCo and Greenlane Holdings, Inc. announced they had signed an agreement to merge in an all stock transaction where KushCo shareholders would receive about 0.2546 shares of GNLN for every share of KSHB. The day of the announcement

GNLN rose 29.7% to close at $5.305 on volume of 17.2 million shares, which was more than the 16.3 million shares outstanding at that time. KSHB also rose but by a more modest 7.9% on the day of the announcement. The day prior to the announcement KushCo had a market capitalization of $181 million.

Greenlane Holdings, Inc. shareholders will own about 50.1% of the combined company, which will retain the name and GNLN symbol. The merged company is expected to have revenue of $310-$330 million for the year ended December 31, 2021.

Summary

This chapter featured five publicly held providers of ancillary products and services that do not touch the plant. Funding from Innovative Industrial properties has been a lifeline for many of the cash starved fully integrated companies and a homerun for IIPR investors.

Fully integrated cannabis companies have also been heavily dependent on the expertise and products offered by Scotts Miracle-Gro, Hydrofarm, and Grow Generation. Without those providers of ancillary services cannabis companies would have had serious cultivation issues. The fully integrated companies also needed the expertise and product solutions offered by Greenlane and KushCo.

Of the companies presented in this chapter, Innovative Industrial Properties stands out as the provider that carved out the most lucrative niche. Scotts Miracle-Gro certainly has the financial wherewithal likely to increase significantly the sales and profits it garners from the cannabis sector as it increasing concentrates its efforts.

Time will tell if GrowGeneration is able to generate the profits and cash flow expected by its shareholders or if the short sellers are correct. Similarly, it remains to be seen if Hydrofarm and the newly merged Greenlane can escape the red ink of net income and cash flow.

CHAPTER 4

OTHER CANNABIS INVESTMENT VEHICLES

Exchange-traded-funds (ETFs) and cannabis focused special purpose acquisition companies (SPACs) have emerged as two other ways to invest in the publicly held cannabis sector. They deserve special attention because of their unique characteristics.

Exchange Traded Funds – ETFs

An ETF is similar to a mutual fund in that it is organized and managed by a fund management company which earns fees from operating the fund. The sponsoring fund company is responsible for marketing, maintaining books and records, selecting investments, and filing required reports with the Securities Exchange Commission (SEC) which is the official regulatory authority.

Like a mutual fund a fund sponsor prepares a prospectus that must be approved by the SEC. The prospectus details the type of investments the fund intends to make. Cannabis ETFs state they are non-diversified since they intend to have a portfolio concentrated with investments in cannabis companies.

At the end of every trading day an ETF, just like a mutual fund, must calculate and publish its net asset value (NAV). The NAV per share is computed by dividing the value of the portfolio by the total number of ETF shares outstanding. Expenses and fees, including management and distribution fees, if any, are accrued daily and taken into account for purposes of determining NAV. When determining NAV, the value of an ETF securities portfolio is based on closing market prices of the securities.

Unlike frequent trading of shares of a traditional open-end mutual fund's shares, frequent trading of shares of an ETF on the secondary market does not disrupt portfolio management, increase trading costs, lead to realization of capitalization gains, or otherwise harm ETF shareholders because these trades do not involve the ETF directly.

Shares of ETFs that invest in the cannabis sector are listed on the NYSE and NASDAQ exchanges. Individual shares may only be bought and sold in the secondary market through brokers at market prices, rather than NAV. Because ETF shares trade at market prices rather than NAV, shares may trade at a price greater than NAV (premium) or less than NAV (discount).

An ETF issues and redeems shares at NAV only in large blocks known as "Creation Units," which only authorized participants (APs), which are typically broker-dealers, may purchase or redeem. An ETF generally issues and redeems Creation Units in exchange for a portfolio of securities and/or a designated amount of U.S. cash. Moreover, an ETF imposes transaction fees on in-kind purchases and redemptions of Creation Units to cover the custodial and other costs incurred by the Fund in effecting in-kind trades. These fees increase if an investor substitutes cash in part or in whole for Creation Units, reflecting the fact that the ETF trading costs increase in those circumstances.

Except when aggregated in Creation Units, ETF shares are not redeemable securities. Once created, ETF shares trade in the secondary market in quantities less than a Creation Unit.

The ability of authorized participants to purchase and redeem shares of an ETF ensures that any premium of discount to NAV will not get too high. If an ETF was selling at a significant discount (market price below NAV) APs would buy enough shares to form a creation unit and present it for redemption in cash.

Investors may incur costs attributable to the difference between the price a buyer is willing to pay to purchase ETF shares (bid) and the price a seller is willing to accept for ETF shares (ask) when buying or selling ETF shares in the secondary market (the "bid-ask spread"). This spread is generally large for cannabis ETFs which do not normally have large average daily trading volumes. As a result, all trades should be entered as limit orders. Investors may also incur customary brokerage commissions and charges on any ETF transactions.

ETF Advantages

A cannabis ETF offers an investor many meaningful advantages over purchasing stocks in specific cannabis companies. The cannabis sector is relatively new and has many unproven companies. In fact, as noted in earlier chapters most are losing money and have negative cash flows. In such situations it is generally recommended that investors diversify by investing in several different companies, which is exactly what an ETF accomplishes. The old adage to not put all your eggs in one basket certainly applies to new economic sectors where investors lack knowledge and historical information.

ETFs have professional money managers making buy and sell decisions. It is generally believed portfolio managers have a depth of knowledge and information that is not available to the average investor. Furthermore, ETF fees are normally below those charged by mutual funds and certainly below 2% management fee and 20% of any appreciation that hedge funds normally charge.

Unlike individual cannabis companies that trade on the over-the-counter (OTC) market in the United States and the Canadian Securities Exchange (CSE), cannabis ETFs are listed and trade on the NYSE and NASDAQ, which have stricter requirements than the NYSE. ETFs which are listed on the NYSE can own actual shares of only cannabis companies like Innovative Industrial Properties, GrowGeneration, Scotts Miracle-Gro, Canopy Growth, Tilray, Cronos, Aurora Cannabis, Jazz, and others that do not "touch the plant in the USA." ETFs, however, cannot own actual shares of U.S. companies like Curaleaf, Green Thumb, Trulieve, et cetera.

Instead, an ETF with the latter companies in their portfolio enters into SWAP contracts with brokerage firms for a given number of shares. SWAP contacts are monitored by a custodian bank to assure proper collateralization of the contracts. A SWAP contract represents ownership by the ETF of a specific number of shares of stock.

An overlooked advantage of cannabis ETFs is the fact that they can also have listed put and call options. A call option is a contract to buy 100 shares of an ETF at a specific price on or before a specific date.

Investors who believe the market price of the ETF will rise may decide to buy a call option, since the cost is a fraction of what it would cost to buy 100 shares. If investors wanted to bet that cannabis stocks will fall then they could buy a put. If these investors' bets were wrong then they would stand to lose all the money they paid for their options.

Options could also be used to hedge a portfolio of cannabis stocks against a possible decline by buying puts on an ETF highly correlated with an investor's portfolio. A person with a portfolio of cannabis stocks could also create yield by selling puts on an ETF that is highly correlated with their portfolio.

An investor with only Canadian cannabis stocks should avoid using an ETF with only U.S. cannabis companies as a hedge; and an investor whose portfolio was composed of only U.S. cannabis companies should avoid hedging with an ETF which has a portfolio heavily weighted with Canadian cannabis companies. Trading in options on cannabis ETFs is very light. Bid-ask spreads are very large; therefore, investors need to enter only limit orders.

Cannabis ETFs

Exhibit 4.1 shows eleven cannabis ETFs listed on the major exchanges in descending order of asset size. POTX is listed on the NASDAQ, TOKE is listed on the BATS, and the other nine are all listed on the NYSE. Three of the ETFs, MJ, MJUS, and MJXL are in the ETF Managers Group (ETFMG) fund management family, while two, YOLO and MSOS, are in the AdvisorShares family. The date each began trading is shown revealing that with the exception of MJ all are of recent origin. All of these ETFs have total fees of 75 basis points (0.0075) or less making them very economical for investors.

Exhibit 4.1
Cannabis ETFs
(July 9, 2021)

ETF Name	Symbol	Inception Date
ETFMG Alternative Harvest ETF	MJ	12/2/2015
AdvisorShares Pure US Cannabis ETF	MSOS	9/1/2020
AdvisorShares Pure Cannabis ETF	YOLO	4/17/2019
Global X Cannabis ETF	POTX	9/17/2019
Cannabis ETF	THCX	7/9/2019
Amplify Seymor Cannabis ETF	CNBS	7/23/2019
Microsectors Cannabis ETF	MJJ	12/13/2019
Cambria Cannabis ETF	TOKE	7/25/2019
Microsectors Cannabis 2X Leveraged ETN	MJO	12/10/2019
ETFMG U.S. Alternative Harvest ETF	MJUS	5/12/2021
ETFMG Alternative Harvest ETF 2X	MJXL	7/7/2021

ETF Managers Group Cannabis ETFs

The ETF Managers Group was the first to introduce a cannabis ETF when it listed ETFMG Alternative Harvest ETF (MJ) on December 2, 2015. That ETF is the largest cannabis ETF with $1.5+ billion in assets as of June 30, 2021.

MJ was designed to track the Prime Alternative Harvest Index which is composed of companies that generate at least half of their revenue from cannabis-related activity although that definition is stretched to pharmaceutical companies that use cannabinoids in medical research, agricultural companies that produce plant cultivation equipment and tobacco manufacturers.

Exhibit 4.2 shows that MJ is heavily weighted with Canadian cannabis companies, but its largest holding is GrowGeneration, a U.S. provider of ancillary products which was discussed in Chapter 3. The top 10 holdings account for 57.9% of the total assets in the MJ portfolio as of July 9, 2021.

Average daily trading volume in MJ is about 950,000 shares. It exhibits significant price volatility as shown by the fact that since it began trading in 2016, MJ has traded as high as $45.40 on September 19, 2018 and as low as $8.81 on March 18, 2020. Its volatility mirrored closely the volatility of the Canadian LPs during MJ's first few years of existence, but that correlation has diminished noticeably as MJ has reduced its concentration of Canadian LP stock holdings.

In response to growing competition in the cannabis ETF space, ETF Managers Group on May 12, 2021 introduced a U.S. version of its highly successful MJ fund giving it the MJUS symbol. A few months later on July 7, 2021 it introduced a leveraged version of its MJ fund with the symbol MJXL.

Exhibit 4.2
MJ Top 10 Holdings
(July 9, 2021)

Cannabis Company	Symbol	% of Total Assets
Growgeneration	GRWG	9.73%
Tilray	TLRY	8.92%
Canopy Growth	CGC	7.56%
Aurora Cannabis	ACB	6.37%
Cronos	CRON	6.37%
Hexo	HEXO	4.34%
OrganiGram	OGI	4.10%
Village Farms	VFF	3.95%
Arena Pharmaceuticals	ARNA	3.44%
Jazz Pharmaceuticals	JAZZ	3.16%

Like all other 2X leveraged ETFs, MJXL is designed to magnify gains by twice the percentage achieved by MJ; unfortunately, MJXL also magnifies losses in MJ. Leveraged products such as MJXL should only be used for short periods of time. Leveraged products have an inherent weakness that guarantees they will approach zero within a few years in a stagnant or declining market.

AdvisorShares Cannabis ETFs

AdvisorShares was the second fund management company to sponsor a cannabis ETF when it introduced YOLO on September 1, 2019. It is the third largest cannabis ETF and had approximately $400 million in total assets in mid 2021. YOLO was the first actively managed cannabis ETF and is designed to fully-invest for pure cannabis exposure. It seeks long-term capital appreciation by investing in both domestic and foreign cannabis equity securities.

YOLO has exhibited significant volatility since it began trading. It traded as low as $5.65 on March 18, 2020 and as high as $31.87 on February 10, 2021. At mid-year 2021 its average daily trading volume was only about 120,000 shares; therefore, investors needed to use limit orders to protect from paying way too much or receiving way too little in transactions.

On September 1, 2020 AdvisorShares introduced its MSOS cannabis ETF at an IPO price of $25. MSOS is an actively managed exchange-traded fund that invests at least 80% of its net assets in securities of companies that derive at least 50% of their net revenue from the marijuana and hemp business in the United States and in derivatives that have economic characteristics similar to such securities. At least 25% of MSOS investments are in the pharmaceuticals, biotechnology and life sciences industry group within the health care sector.

MSOS is non-diversified and may invest a greater percentage of its assets in a particular issuer than a diversified fund. A high percentage of MSOS assets are invested in cannabis companies operating throughout the United States. A company operating in more that one state is known as a multi-state-operator (MSO).

YOLO and MSOS are both listed on the NYSE. Because of listing requirements, all holdings of shares of companies operating in the U.S. are in the form of SWAP contracts with regulated broker-dealers.

The introduction of MSOS by AdvisorShares coincided with a surge in demand for U.S. cannabis companies dubbed multi-state-operators. The demand for shares of U.S. multi-state-operators was promulgated by a flurry of mergers and acquisitions and accompanying media exposure fanning investor dreams of wealth. The surge in interest reached its peak about a month after the Georgia Senate runoffs that allowed the Democrats to take control of the Senate. The prevailing belief was the Democrats would deschedule cannabis and remove the onerous IRC Section 280E.

In that environment attracted huge amounts of money and within months of its introduction it reached $1 billion in assets under management (AUM). The fact that it attracted all that new money to the cannabis sector led directly to higher prices of stocks it acquired directly or indirectly via SWAP contracts.

Prior to the introduction of its MSOS ETF, AdvisorShares had a total of less that $800 million in AUM in all their other funds combined. The successful launch of MSOS has been widely heralded and the size of its holdings makes it a force in the U.S. cannabis sector.

MSOS has exhibited the same notable volatility as the cannabis sector. During its first nine months of existence, it traded as high as $55.91 on February 10, 2021 and as low as $20.45 on September 24, 2020. Its average daily trading volume amounted to about 500,000 shares in mid-2021.

Exhibit 4.3 shows the top 10 holdings of MSOS and Exhibit 4.4 shows the top 10 for YOLO. MSOS has total assets of approximately $1 billion.

The top 10 holdings in MSOS account for 75.6% of its total assets. The top 10 for YOLO account for 72.4%. A look at these percentages lets investors know what they own. For example, 12.95% of a single share of MSOS would be composed of Green Thumb stock, 11.77% by Curaleaf, et cetera.

Exhibit 4.3
AdvisorShares Top 10 Holdings
(July 9, 2021)

MSOS Cannabis Company	Symbol	% of Total Assets	YOLO Cannabis Company	Symbol	% of Total Assets
Green Thumb	GTBIF	12.95%	Village Farms	VFF	14.63%
Curaleaf	CURLF	11.77%	Innovative Industrial	IIPR	10.70%
Trulieve	TCNNF	10.89%	Green Thumb	GTBIF	6.97%
Cresco Labs	CRLBF	9.44%	GrowGeneration	GRWG	6.79%
Ayr Wellness	AYRWF	7.13%	Curaleaf	CURLF	6.04%
Terrascend	TRSSF	6.46%	Canopy Growth	CGC	5.88%
Innovative Industrial	IIPR	4.42%	Tilray	TLRY	5.88%
Harvest Health	HRVSF	4.38%	Harvest Health	HRVSF	5.49%
Columbia Care	CCHWF	4.14%	Cresco Labs	CRLBF	5.06%
GrowGeneration	GRWG	4.06%	Trulieve	TCNNF	4.96%

Green Thumb, Curaleaf, Trulieve, and Cresco are the top four holdings of MSOS and have been since the ETF was launched. The top three have changed positions as various times; however, they have always accounted individually for more that 10% of MSOS AUM. As a group, the top three have always accounted for at least 1/3rd of AUM. These are clearly core holdings and unlikely to be sold in the event of a need to raise cash even though they are far more liquid that other holdings.

The MSOS portfolio since inception had included about 30 holdings and the portfolio manager has demonstrated a willingness to add companies, totally liquidate others, and alter the percentage of AUM devoted to particular companies. The only companies that have been totally liquidated from MSOS are PerkinElmer, Zynerba Pharmaceuticals, and Arena Pharmaceuticals.

MSOS had holdings in 13 cannabis companies that individually accounted for less that 1% of its total assets. When totaled, the 13 accounted for only 5.4% of the assets. Holdings of Goodness Growth amounted to 0.78% of MSOS AUM, Power REIT 0.74%, C21 Investments 0.70%, Lowell Farms 0.59%, Charlotte's Web 0.45%, Canopy River 0.36%, Gaege Growth 0.34%, Mercer Park Brand 0.34%, Ceres 0.32%, Vext Science 0.31%, cbdMd 0.22%, Greenland Holdings 0.16%, and Hempfusion Wellness 0.13%.

YOLO and MSOS are designed to pay dividends. They are able to pay dividends because some of their holdings, such as Innovative Industrial Properties, pay them dividends. MSOS also earns fees by lending securities.

In 2020 YOLO paid dividends of $0.1262 per share on March 31; $0.1075 on June 30; $0.0737 on September 30; and $0.0373 on December 31. Those dividends totaled $0.3447 and represented a yield of 2.0% based on YOLO's year end closing price of $17.

Other Cannabis ETFs

The other six cannabis ETFs shown in Exhibit 4.1 all had less than $200 million in total assets on June 30, 2021. Asset size is important, since fixed costs incurred by a fund sponsor are significant. It is in the best interests of people to invest in funds that render profits to fund sponsors who can then afford to absorb fund expenses that might otherwise have to be allocated to shareholders. It is not unusual for fund sponsors to liquidate funds when it becomes apparent that they cannot reach a break-even point. In such a situation, shareholders do not lose money but it is inconvenient and may have tax consequences.

Special Purpose Acquisition Company (SPAC)

A special purpose acquisition company (SPAC) is a shell corporation listed on a stock exchange formed strictly to raise funds to finance a merger or acquisition within a set time frame. They are also known as "blank check" companies and have become incredibly prominent in recent years especially in the United States cannabis sector.

Blank check companies have been associated with numerous fraudulent schemes over the centuries and rightfully earned notorious reputations. In 1990 the U.S. Congress enacted the Penny Stock Reform Act to clamp down on fraud in unlisted so-called penny stocks, which typically trade below $5 per share on the over-the-counter (OTC) market.

In 1992 the SEC enacted Rule 419 imposing significant safeguards in connection with shares of a blank check companies. These safeguards included requiring almost all funds raised and shares issued to be placed in escrow pending a merger; imposing an eighteen-month time limit to complete a merger; mandating investor reconfirmation of an investment prior to a merger, and other stipulations.

On May 6, 2008 the SEC approved a NYSE rule enabling it to list SPACs. Prior to that date, SPACs were confined to trading on the OTC Bulletin Board and the American Stock Exchange. Exhibit 4.4 shows that the number of SPAC IPOs from 2016 through mid 2021 has exploded.

Exhibit 4.4
U.S. SPAC IPOs: 2016-2021
June 30, 2021

Year	Number of New SPACs	Gross Proceeds ($ in billions)	Average Size ($ in millions)
2021	366	112.7	307.9
2020	248	83.4	335.3
2019	59	23.6	230.5
2018	46	10.8	233.7
2017	34	10.0	295.5
2016	13	3.5	269.2

Cannabis SPAC

A cannabis SPAC is no different from any other SPAC. Both must follow the SEC and exchange rules. To fully appreciate a cannabis SPAC it seems beneficial to look at an actual one from its formation through its IPO. The only thing missing from the following SPAC is the absence of a PPE or private-to-public equity infusion of cash, which is likely attributable to the classification of cannabis at a Class I Scheduled substance and the fact that most institutional investors have decided to avoid the cannabis sector until there is some meaningful legislation at the Federal level.

The only cannabis SPAC to announce a pipe transaction is Ceres Acquisition Corp. It stated that when it closes its qualifying transaction with Parallel it will also close on a $225 million over-subscribed PIPE led by Ceres and Parallel. Investors in that PIPE will receive 22.5 million units at $10 per unit, which is the same price paid by original investors in the Ceres IPO.

Cannabis Strategies Acquisition Corporation

On July 31, 2017 Cannabis Strategies Acquisition Corporation (CSAC) was incorporated under the Business Corporations Act of Ontario where it is domiciled. On that date it began operations as a SPAC with an expressed purpose of effecting an acquisition of one or more businesses or assets, by way of a merger, amalgamation, arrangement, share exchange, asset acquisition, share purchase, reorganization, or any other similar business combination.

Every SPAC is free to merge with any business; however, most express a preference for a particular industry. In announcing its formation CSAC stated it intended to focus on searching for target businesses in marijuana production, distribution, and/or related sectors.

On November 13, 2017 CSAC filed a prospectus for its initial public offering (IPO). The IPO was for C$125 million. It entailed the issuance of 12.5 million Class a Restricted Voting Units at an offering price of C$10 per unit. Each unit consisted of one Class A restricted Voting Share, one Warrant, and one Right. Upon the IPO closing each Class A Restricted Voting Share was automatically converted into one Class B Share. The Warrants and Rights were immediately detached at the time of the IPO and became freely tradeable.

The warrants with an exercise price of C$11.50 became exercisable 65 days after CSAC consummated a closing "Qualifying" transaction. The warrants are set to expire five years after closing the qualifying transaction. Rights can be converted into Class B shares immediately after the qualify transaction closes with 10 rights being required for each Class B share with no additional consideration required.

Regulations stipulate that a SPAC has two years to enter into a qualifying transaction, which is defined as a transaction in which 80% of the SPAC funds are used; however, shareholders can vote to grant an extension. If there is no qualifying transaction within that stipulated or amended time frame then all funds raised from IPO investors must be returned with interest from the escrow account where they are required to be kept until used in a qualifying transaction.

On October 17, 2018 CSAC announced a proposed qualifying transaction. That transaction then had to be approved by owners of the IPO units at a special meeting. Holders of Class A Restricted Voting Shares were entitled to redeem all or a portion of their shares regardless of whether they voted for or against or did not vote on the transaction. Furthermore, warrant and rights holders were entitled to keep those even if they redeemed their shares.

CSAC closed on its qualifying transaction on May 24, 2019 when it acquired five companies named Washoe, LivFree, Canopy, Sira, and CannaPunch. On that same date it changed its name to Ayr Strategies Inc. and its Ayr Class B stock, Ayr rights, and Ayr warrants began trading on the NEO exchange. Seven months elapsed from the time CSAC announced its qualifying transaction until it closed, and the closing was only a month shy of the two-year window for a SPAC to consummate a qualifying transaction.

The organizers of the CSAC SPAC who are officially known as "Sponsors" enjoyed a very significant increase in their personal net worths as a result of incorporating the SPAC and buying some cannabis companies. Immediately after the IPO, and after the investment bankers exercised their over allotment option "the green shoe," the sponsor Mercer Park CB, L.P. owned 3,662,110 "Founders' Shares" for which it paid C$25,010 or C$0.00683 per share. Those shares as of July 9, 2021 were worth $106.3 million.

In addition to the founders shares the organizers gave themselves an option to acquire 2,734,375 warrants (assuming exercise of green shoe) for C$1 per warrant allowing them to acquire shares at C$11.50 per share for the next five years. On July 9, 2021 those warrants could be sold for a profit of $53.1 million.

The founders also reserved for themselves and bought 273,438 of the IPO units for C$10 per unit. Each of those units with warrants and rights would now be worth about $52.09 million or a total of $14.2 million, so the sponsor would have a profit of about $12.1 million.

If you add all the above realizable profits available to the Mercer Park CB, L.P., the sponsor, it amounts to $171.5 million on an initial investment of $2.1 million. So, they made 81.7x their investment in 43 months and their CAGR was about 283%. The CSAC SPAC has been a success since it went public, so the above assumed realizable profit of $171.7 million needs to be compared with the approximately $494.6 million IPO investors have made since it went public. Then again, chances are the IPO buyers were heavily weighted by family and friends of Mercer Park CB, L.P.

SPAC Issue Similarities

Sponsors of SPACs essentially get a carried interest for forming a corporation designed to acquire other companies. That carried interest is generally at least a 20% ownership of the SPAC common shares plus warrants plus right to cheaply buy more shares.

A number of academic studies suggest that SPACs have performed poorly after closing their qualifying transactions. There is also some anecdotal evidence suggesting that a surge in SPAC formation tends to create inordinately high valuations for private companies especially when SPAC formation is concentrated in an industry. This concern is certainly present in the cannabis sector which has seen a surge in SPAC formation.

The Cannabis SPAC Universe

Exhibit 4.5 lists all known publicly held cannabis companies that are either SPACs or started out as SPACs. They are listed in the chronological order of their SPAC IPOs.

As previously mentioned, Ayr Wellness began its corporate life as Cannabis Strategies Acquisition Corporation, which was a SPAC. Akerna resulted from a qualifying transaction whereby the SPAC MTech Acquisiton Corp merged with MJ Freeway. Columbia Care emerged as a result of a qualifying transaction the SPAC Canaccord Genuity Growth Corp. The Parent Company evolved as the qualifying transaction for the SPAC Subversive Capital Acquisition Corp. Vintage Wine Estates was the name assumed when the SPAC Bespoke Capital Acquisition used it as its qualifying transaction.

Six of the 19 SPACs listed in Exhibit 4.5 have consummated their qualifying transactions as of June 30, 2021. Three other SPACs have announced agreements and are awaiting all the necessary approvals. Included in those three SPACs are Mercer Park which has an agreement with Glass House; Ceres which has an agreement with Parallel; and Greenrose which has an agreement with several companies.

Ten SPACs listed in Exhibit 4.5 have completed their IPO and received funds which are now in escrow. The two-year time period ran out on Tuscan Holdings on January 16, 2021 and it had to get an extension from shareholders, which it did until September 3, 2021.

The same clock is getting set to run out on Merida Merger which has a two-year deadline of October 7, 2021. The last six SPACs listed in Exhibit 4.5 still have at least a year to shop for a suitable qualifying transaction.

The 19 SPACs in Exhibit 4.5 raised a total of $3.44 billion in their IPOs. The largest raise was $575 million by Subversive, followed by Mercer Park at $402.5, Bespoke at $380 million, and Silver Spike II at $250 million. While these numbers appear large to the average person, they are very small compared to the $323 billion raised by all SPACs in the same period of time and shown previously in Exhibit 4.4. Of the billions flowing into SPACs only about 1% is finding its way into the cannabis space.

Exhibit 4.5
Cannabis SPACs: 2017-June 30, 2021

Cannabis SPACs	Symbol	IPO Date	IPO Amount	IPO Price	Qualifying Trans Date	Qualifying Trans Price	Stock Price High	Stock Price Low	Stock Price 6/30/21	Deadline Date
Cannabis Stategies Acquisition/Ayr Wellness	AYRWF	12/17/2017	C125	C10.00	5/24/19	16.60	37.50	4.65	28.50	12/17/2019
Mtech Acquisition/Akerna	KERN	1/30/2018	50.0	10.00	6/17/19	11.99	72.65	2.17	4.03	1/18/2018
Canacord Genuity Growth Corp/Columbia Care	CCHWF	9/20/2018	C46	C3.00	4/26/19	6.51	7.89	0.78	4.64	9/18/2018
Mercer Park Brand Acquisition Corp	MRCQF	5/13/2019	402.5	10.00	4/8/2021*	10.04	13.99	9.66	12.20	5/13/2021
Subversive Capital Acquisition/The Parent Co	GRAMF	7/16/2019	575.0	10.00	1/14/21	13.96	13.96	5.10	5.58	7/16/2021
Tuscan Holdings Corp II	THCA	7/16/2019	172.5	10.00			11.48	9.20	10.05	1/16/2021
Silver Spike Acquisition Corp/WM Technology	MAPS	8/7/2019	125.0	10.00	6/9/21	17.25	29.50	9.51	17.86	8/7/2021
Bespoke Capital Acquisition Corp/Vintage Wine	VWE	8/15/2019	380.0	10.00	6/7/21	11.07	13.48	9.25	12.00	8/15/2021
Merida Merger Corp I	MCMJ	11/7/2019	120.0	10.00			11.24	8.56	9.95	11/7/2021
Stable Road Acquisition Corporation	SRAC	11/13/2019	172.5	10.00			29.18	9.20	13.97	5/13/2021
Greenrose Acquisition Corp	GNRS	2/13/2020	150.0	10.00	3/15/2021*	10.08	11.46	9.61	9.99	8/13/2021
Ceres Acquisititon Corp	CERAF	3/3/2020	120.0	10.00	2/22/2021*	11.45	15.00	9.31	10.10	12/3/2022
Ackrell SPAC Partners I Company	ACKIU	12/21/2020	138.0	10.00			11.00	10.00	10.23	6/21/2022
BGP Acquisition Corp	BGPPF	2/4/2021	115.0	10.00			10.00	9.48	9.80	2/4/2023
Tuatara Capital Acquisition Corp	TCAC	2/12/2021	175.0	10.00			9.84	9.63	9.70	2/12/2023
Choice Consolidation Corp	CDXXF	2/19/2021	172.5	10.00			10.10	9.75	10.00	2/19/2023
Silver Spike Acquisition Corp II	SPKB	3/11/2021	250.0	10.00			10.05	9.69	9.75	3/11/2023
Silver Spike III Acquisition Corp.	SPKC.UN.U	5/27/2021	125.0	10.00						5/27/2023
Northern Lights Acquisition Corp	NLITU	6/28/2021	115.0	10.00						6/28/2023
Clover Leaf Capital	CLOEU		125.0	10.00						

Note: * is date qualifying deal was announced

Exhibit 4.5 shows that all the SPAC IPOs were priced at $10 USD except for the two Canadian offerings. Share prices are given for the day a qualifying transaction was closed or the day an agreement was announced but not yet closed. The highest and lowest prices at which individual stocks traded are shown along with the closing prices on June 30, 2021.

A review of the prices shows significant volatility in the share prices of Ayr Wellness, Akerna, Columbia Care, and WM Technology. The observed volatility in older SPACs is not different from that observed in cannabis stocks in general during the past three years. Cannabis investors have certainly experienced the thrill of victory and the agony of defeat as waves of euphoria and gloom spread throughout the sector.

A quick glance at the IPO prices and the closing prices on June 30, 2021 reveals that great shareholder wealth has not been created by cannabis SPACs. The same cannot be said for the sponsors who captured 20% of the $3.4 billion invested in cannabis SPACs.

It remains to be seen if the SPAC sponsors add any value by using other people's money to go shopping for vertically integrated cannabis companies and providers of ancillary products and services to cannabis companies. The fact that SPAC sponsors are allowed raise funds by making projections based on very few if any observations is a license to steal without any liability. Investors who believe sponsors are financial wizards with unique dashboard controls that allow them to makes massive amounts of money are likely to be rudely surprised.

Stable Road Acquisition Corporation

An examination of Stable Road Acquisition Corporation is worthwhile because it illuminates a number of problems associated with SPACs. Its headquarters are in Venice, California and on October 29, 2029 it filed an S-1 with the SEC as a newly organized blank check company (SPAC). Stable stated it was formed for the purpose of effecting a merger, capital stock exchange, asset acquisition, stock purchase, reorganization or similar business combination with one or more businesses. It went on to state that while it had not selected any target it intended to focus its search on companies in the cannabis industry.

Its initial public offering (IPO) consisted of 15 million units at an offering price of $10.00. Each unit consisted of one share of our Class A common stock and one-half of one redeemable warrant. Only whole warrants were exercisable and allowed the purchase of one share of Class A common stock at a price of $11.50 per share. The underwriters exercised an option to acquire an additional 2,250,000 units at the $10 offering price, and that brought the gross proceeds of the IPO to $172.5 million.

Purchasers of IPO units were given the opportunity to redeem all or a portion of their shares of the Class A common stock upon the completion of Stable Road's initial business combination. If Stable Road did not complete its qualifying transaction within 18 months from the closing of its IPO, it stated it would redeem 100% of the public shares for cash. Its IPO closed on November 13, 2019.

After the money was raised and put in escrow, the sponsors of the Stable Road SPAC decided, for unknown reasons, to focus their "unique" talents outside the cannabis industry. They, instead, decided to pursue a qualifying transaction with Momentus, an in-space transportation company. Completion of that transaction could not occur within the 18-month deadline, so on May 13 Stable Road barely got a three-month extension approved when 66.2% of the shareholders casting votes approved the extension. The required approval was 65%. Fittingly, the CEO thanked the shareholders for their "overwhelming support."

As might be expected, the stock price of Stable Road exhibited considerable volatility following its IPO. SRAC traded as high as $ 29.18 on February 10, 2021 and as low as $9.20 on March 19, 2020.

A large number of class action lawsuits have been filed against Stable Road sponsors seemingly related to a Momentus announcement on May 11, 2021 that the Federal Aviation Administration (FAA) denied its payload review application. The denial apparently stems from an interagency review concluding that the launch of Momentus payload poses national security concerns.

The fact that sponsors of this SPAC decided their expertise allowed them to flip a switch and focus on space travel is troubling. It speaks volumes about SPACs and the gullibility of investors.

It is not surprising that the SEC on July 13, 2021 announced charges against Stable Road Acquisition, its sponsor SRC-NI, and its CEO. In announcing the charges, SEC Chairman Gary Gensler said this case illustrates the inherent risks of SPAC transactions caused because sponsors who stand to receive significant profits lose sight of their fiduciary duty. SRAC dropped 10.3% from $11.88 to $10.66 on 5x normal daily volume the day following the announcement.

Summary

This chapter has shown that, instead of buying individual companies, investors can buy a portfolio of cannabis companies by buying shares in cannabis ETFs. The small percentage fee charged by professional managers makes investing in cannabis ETFs a no brainer for investors with limited sums of money. Furthermore, the investment graveyard is littered with the corpses of part time investors who failed to diversify their investments because of a lack of funds.

Just imagine how goofy the investment world really is. Let's say you have $100 that you want to invest in the cannabis space and you have only two choices.

You can give it to an investment specialist who devotes 100% of his knowledge, time and energy to studying perhaps 500 cannabis companies; and, he will report daily to you on how your investment is performing. He will charge you no more than a $0.75 for his services.

On the other hand, you can chose to give your $100 to some Wall Street expert who claims expertise in horticulture, accounting, finance, marketing, law, and human relations; but has never grown a tomato or an herb. If you give this expert your $100, they will use it to buy a cannabis company. After they buy that company you will own 80% of it and they will own 20%, because you hired them to buy it.

It's your decision and your money!

CHAPTER 5

CHEAPEST TO MOST EXPENSIVE CANNABIS STOCKS

It is generally accepted that the intrinsic value of a company equals the discounted present value of free cash flow generated in the current and future years. If intrinsic values are calculated for all companies in a sector then those companies can be ranked from the most to the least valuable.

Once the value of a company has been calculated then the value of a share of stock can be easily calculated. It is the value of the company divided by the number of shares. If there was only one share of stock then that share would equal the total value of the company. As the number of shares increases the percentage of ownership represented by a single share decreases.

If the intrinsic value of a company increases by 50% and the number of shares outstanding increases by more than 50% the intrinsic value of a share of stock will decline. Of course, if the intrinsic value of a company increases by a greater percentage than the shares outstanding then the intrinsic value of a share of stock will increase.

This fundamental maxim of investing is why investors like Warren Buffett prefer to own shares in companies that are actually reducing the number of shares they have outstanding. As companies buyback shares, his ownership position and claim on future cash flows rises in proportion to the percentage decline in outstanding shares.

The Problem Valuing Cannabis Company Stocks

A serious valuation problem occurs, however, when companies do not produce positive operating cash flow. In such instances, security analysts will use a host of other metrics to assess valuation and justify share prices. They will compare share price to earnings, operating income, sales revenue, book value, tangible book value, financial leverage, and EBITA for companies and sectors to determine relative values within and among sectors.

By so doing, they seek to identify which company's stock is cheap or expensive compared to others within a sector and which sectors are cheap or expensive relative to other sectors.

The problem of identifying value is compounded when there is not enough historical financial information to prepare statistically significant forecasts of revenue and expenses. This is exactly the problem that faces investors in the cannabis sector, since it is only a few years old. Accordingly, investors have to rely on static measures that use available financial information to help them make informed investment decisions.

Valuation Metrics

Exhibit 5.1 shows eight valuation metrics for 33 vertically integrated U.S. cannabis companies that operated throughout 2020. The share price of each company is expressed as a multiple of the per share amounts of operating cash flow, adjusted operating cash flow, net income after taxes, book value, tangible book value, adjusted operating income, Adjusted EBITDA, and total revenue. All calculations were made using audited financial information presented in company annual reports filed with the SEC and SEDAR for the fiscal year 2020.

The number of shares used in all calculations is the number of common shares that companies reported as outstanding on December 31, 2020. A lack of readily available detailed information prohibited a precise determination of the number of diluted shares outstanding at the end of 2020.

The Operating Cash Flow metric was calculated by dividing a company's share price by the quotient of cash provided by operations divided by shares outstanding. The Tax Adjusted Operating Cash Flow metric takes into consideration current income taxes incurred in 2020 but not paid by the company. A company that does not pay its current income taxes increases its reported cash provided by operations by the amount of the nonpayment, which it books as an increase in a current liability labeled income taxes payable. The third valuation metric shown in Exhibit 5.1 is the share price expressed as a multiple of net income after taxes per share and is generally referred to as the PE ratio.

The fourth valuation metric in Exhibit 5.1 shows share price as a multiple of book value per share, and book value is the amount by which assets exceed liabilities. The fifth valuation metric, tangible book value, simply subtracts goodwill and intangible assets from book value or shareholders' equity.

The sixth valuation metric shown in Exhibit 5.1 is share price as a multiple of adjusted operating income. Cannabis companies that use IFRS accounting include in operating income realized fair value amounts in inventory sold and unrealized fair value gain on growth of biological assets. Companies that use GAAP accounting do not include those amounts in their operating income; therefore, the impact of biologicals was removed from income statements of IFRS reporting companies to make proper comparisons.

The seventh valuation metric is share price expressed as a multiple of Adjusted EBITDA. Adjusted EBITDA amounts were generally obtained from the Management Discussion and Analysis of Financial Condition and Results of Operation (MD&A) filing that accompanied the Audited Annual Financial Statements filing.

The eighth valuation metric shown in Exhibit 5.1 is share price expressed as a multiple of revenue. The revenue number used was total revenue less any excise taxes.

Data presented in Exhibit 5.1 accurately measure cannabis company stocks at a moment in time. It is a snapshot of share valuations of cannabis companies while they were experiencing rapid growth. As the industry matures and years pass, a series of snapshots will be able to show trends and patterns not revealed by the static analysis mandated by a paucity of historical financial information.

Given this limitation, metrics presented in Exhibit 5.1 do provide an accurate way to evaluate the value of one cannabis company's stock relative to others in the cannabis sector. At the same time, several of these metrics allow cannabis company stocks to be compared to stocks of companies in other industries.

Operating Cash Flow Valuation Metric

Column 3 of Exhibit 5.1 shows that 12 (36.4%) of the 33 seed-to-sale cannabis companies reported positive cash provided by operations. Among those 12, Tilt Holdings had the best metric in that a share of TLLTF traded at 11x its net operating cash flow. It was followed closely by C21 Investments at 16.6x, Next Green Wave at 16.9x, Cansortium at 17.9x, Ayr Wellness at 22.6x, Vext Science at 28.6x, Trulieve at 37.9x, MariMed at 42.8x, Vibe Growth at 53.6x, Green Thumb at 54.5x, Terrascend at 83.0x, and Curaleaf at 643.1x.

None of the top five Canadian LPs and only two of the six providers of ancillary products and services had positive cash provided by operations. Scotts Miracle-Gro stock traded at 24.3x net operating cash flow and Innovative Industrial Properties traded at 43.6x.

The same valuation metric was calculated for six widely followed growth stocks and six consumer package goods stocks. These 12 well-known companies are included because cannabis company observers believe cannabis companies are high growth, consumer package goods companies. Assessing how cannabis company valuations rank relative to these others sectors is important, because cannabis companies are competing with them for investor attention and dollars.

Exhibit 5.1
Valuation Metrics of Vertically Integrated Cannabis Companies for 2020

Company	Symbol	Oper Cash Flow	Tax Adj Oper Cash Flow	NIAT*	Book Value	Tangible Book Value	Adj Oper Income	Adj EBITDA	Total Rev
Curaleaf	CURLF	643.1	NM	NM	5.8	73.1	NM	55.1	12.7
Green Thumb	GTBIF	54.5	59.8	348.6	5.7	41.7	49.3	29.1	9.4
Trulieve	TCNNF	37.9	37.0	60.0	8.4	13.3	17.3	15.1	7.2
Cresco Labs	CRLBF	NM	NM	NM	5.2	49.1	NM	32.7	8.0
Terrascend	TRSSF	83.0	144.4	NM	246.4	NM	120.4	45.6	13.8
Columbia Care	CCHWF	NM	NM	NM	5.2	18.9	NM	NM	9.3
Harvest Health	HRVSF	NM	NM	NM	2.3	NM	NM	57.1	3.8
Chalice Brands Ltd	CHALF	NM	NM	NM	87.7	NM	NM	NM	21.9
Planet 13	PLNHF	NM	NM	NM	8.4	10.9	NM	114.5	14.5
Ayr Wellness	AYRWF	22.6	40.9	NM	5.5	NM	523.1	14.7	5.3
Jushi Holdings	JUSHF	NM	NM	NM	NM	NM	NM	NM	11.0
4Front Ventures	FFNTF	NM	NM	NM	11.6	NM	NM	83.4	8.5
Acreage Holdings	ACRHF	NM	NM	NM	1.3	4.5	NM	NM	2.7
Goodness Holdings	GDNSF	NM	NM	NM	2.7	3.3	NM	NM	3.4
Item 9 Labs	INLB	NM	NM	NM	11.2	33.5	NM	NM	15.4
MariMed	MRMD	42.8	42.8	59.5	17.9	24.6	32.2	8.1	2.8
Tilt Holdings	TLLTF	11.0	8.9	NM	0.4	1.9	NM	6.3	0.7
MedMen	MMNFF	NM	NM	NM	0.4	NM	NM	NM	0.5
Cansortium	CNTMF	17.9	220.9	NM	5.2	NM	NM	14.1	2.8
Red White & Bloom	RWBYF	NM	NM	NM	0.7	3.0	NM	NM	6.4
C21 Investments	CXXIF	16.6	16.1	NM	6.5	NM	NM	16.9	4.6
Next Green Wave	NXGWF	16.9	16.9	14.9	3.0	3.0	24.0	14.9	4.1
Stem Holdings	STMH	NM	NM	NM	1.1	NM	NM	NM	5.6
Harborside	HBORF	NM	NM	NM	4.7	NM	NM	122.0	1.4
Medicine Man	SHWZ	NM	NM	NM	1.5	NM	NM	NM	2.6
Lowell Farms	LOWLF	NM	NM	NM	1.4	1.5	14.6	NM	1.5
Slang Worldwide	SLGWF	NM	NM	NM	1.6	NM	NM	NM	3.9
Vibe Growth	VBSCF	53.6	NM	53.3	3.8	10.9	23.2	13.1	1.6
Vext Science	VEXTF	28.6	28.6	41.8	2.4	3.1	34.0	13.0	3.5
Hollister Bio	HSTRF	NM	NM	NM	9.5	67.4	NM	NM	1.6
Body & Mind	BMMJ	NM	NM	9.2	1.3	6.5	NM	15.9	1.7
iAnthus Capital	ITHUF	NM	NM	NM	0.7	NM	NM	NM	0.2
Plus Products	PLPRF	NM	NM	NM	520.3	2,725.6	NM	NM	1.6

Note: NM is not meaningful and NIAT is net income after taxes

Exhibit 5.2 shows that growth company stocks generally sold at slightly higher multiples of net operating cash flow than consumer package goods (CPG) stocks. Growth stocks (excluding Tesla) sold at an average multiple of 22.7, while CPG stocks sold at an average multiple of 16.0. If Curaleaf is excluded, the average multiple of net operating cash flow at which the other 11 cannabis company stocks sold was 32.1x.

Importantly, all 12 non-cannabis stocks had positive cash provided by operations. By contrast, 63.6% of the vertically integrated and 71.4% of the providers of ancillary services had negative cash flow from operations.

This comparative analysis of cannabis stocks with growth and CPG stocks reveals that cannabis stocks are way overpriced based on cash provided from operations. Of course, this is only one valuation metric and the analysis covered only one year.

Cannabis investors who claim cannabis stocks are undervalued are certainly not looking at company share prices as multiples of the cash provided by company operating activities. Dramatic improvement in this important valuation metric is required for cannabis companies to compete with companies in other sectors in the quest for investment dollars.

Tax Adjusted Operating Cash Flow Valuation Metric

The number of cannabis companies reporting positive cash provided by operations dropped to 10 once the adjustment was made to reflect current income tax payments. Curaleaf reported its cash provided by operation was $12,355,000; however, they failed to pay $57,753,000 in current income taxes and when that adjustment was made Curaleaf's adjusted cash flow became a negative $45,398,000. Similarly, but on a much smaller scale, Vibe Growth's $724,343 positive cash provided by operations became a negative $708,217 when its nonpayment of $1,432,560 was considered.

Exhibit 5.2
Share Price to Net Operating Cash Flow: 2020

Companies	Symbol	Multiple
Tilt Holdings	TLLTF	11.0
C21 Investments	CXXIF	16.6
Next Green Wave	NXGWF	16.9
Cansortium	CNTMF	17.9
Ayr Wellness	AYRWF	22.6
Vext Science	VEXTF	28.6
Trulieve	TCNNF	37.9
MariMed	MRMD	42.8
Vibe Growth	VBSCF	53.6
Green Thumb	GTBIF	54.5
Terrascend	TRSSF	83.0
Curaleaf	CURLF	643.1
Providers		
Scotts Miracle-Gro	SMG	24.3
Innovative Industrial Products	IIPR	43.6
Growth		
Google	GOOG	18.2
Facebook	FB	20.1
Apple	APPL	22.6
Amazon	AMZN	24.8
Microsoft	MSFT	27.8
Tesla	TSLA	114.0
Consumer Package Goods		
Kraft	KHC	8.4
Anheuser-Busch InBev	BUD	12.6
Philip Morris USA	PM	12.8
Pepsicola	PEP	19.0
Proctor & Gamble	PG	19.6
Coca Cola	KO	23.6

Other companies that reported significantly inflated operating cash flow because of nonpayment of income taxes were Cansortium whose cash provided by operations fell from $8,088,000 to a tax adjusted cash flow of $655,000 because it did not pay $7,433,000 in current income taxes; and, Ayr Wellness whose reported $36,511,663 in cash provided by operations dropped to a tax adjusted cash flow of $20,729,000 when adjusted for it not paying of $16,382,580 in current income taxes.

Cansortium's share price to "tax adjusted" operating cash flow soared to 220.9x from 17.9x before adjustment. Ayr Wellness share price to tax adjusted cash flow multiple almost doubled to 40.9x from 22.6x.

Interestingly, Tilt Holdings had the best cash flow metric before and after adjustment. In fact, it and Trulieve stood out because they both paid more in taxes in 2020 than they incurred. Tilt paid $2,289,000 more than it owed and Trulieve paid $2,452,000 more than it owed.

The observed difference in cash flow as a result of such nonpayment by U.S. cannabis companies is very material, since it is their cheapest source of funds. The IRS penalty is only 6% per year for failure to make timely tax payments. Cannabis companies throughout 2020 had to pay double digit rates to obtain funds directly via notes or indirectly via leases; therefore, not paying current income taxes provides cheap money to a cannabis company. At the same time, it allows cannabis companies to surreptitiously inflate their cash flow to make it seem better that it really is.

From a strictly cash flow point of view, looking only at audited cash flow statements, Tilt Holdings shares traded at the lowest multiple at the end of 2020. Other companies that scored well on this metric before and after adjustment were C21 Investments, Next Green Wave, Vext Science, and Trulieve.

Net Income After Taxes Per Share – PE Ratio Valuation Metric

The price-earnings or PE ratio has been the single most used metric by investors to determine the merit of an investment in the past 100 years. It is calculated by dividing a company's stock price by the net income after tax per share. Company's generally calculate their net income per share on the basis of the weighted average number of actual and diluted shares outstanding during the period in which the income was earned. Diluted shares are supposed to include actual shares plus shares issuable from convertible debentures and other securities along with shares issuable for warrants, rights, and options that are in-the-money (ITM) and exercisable. An examination of cannabis company financials suggested the number of fully diluted shares reported by companies were less than the total number of shares that would actually be outstanding if eligible holders of exercisable, in the money securities converted into shares.

As previously mentioned, Exhibit 5.1 was constructed using the actual number of shares outstanding at the end of 2020. PE multiples are, therefore, somewhat lower than they would be if the number of diluted shares was used.

Only seven or 21.2% of the 33 cannabis companies in Exhibit 5.1 reported net income after taxes in 2020. The other 26 cannabis companies or 78.8% reported net losses after taxes.

On the PE valuation metric alone, Body & Mind was the cheapest cannabis company stock at the end of 2020. Body & Mind had the lowest PE multiple at 9.2x and it was followed closely by Next Green Wave at 14.9x. Other company's able to produce PE multiples were Vext Science at 41.8x, Vibe Growth at 53.3x, MariMed at 59.5x, Trulieve at 60.0x, and Green Thumb at 348.6x.

All of the top five Canada LPs and three of the six providers of ancillary products and services reported net losses after taxes in 2020. As a result, PE multiples could only be calculated for Scotts Miracle-Gro, Innovative Industrial Properties, and GrowGeneration. Scotts had a PE multiple of 35.0x, Innovative Industrial had a 58.0x, and GrowGeneration had an astronomical multiple of 574.6x.

A comparison of the PE Ratios of the seven vertically integrated cannabis companies and three providers of ancillary products and services against the 12 well known non cannabis companies is presented in Exhibit 5.3. If the outliers like Green Thumb, GrowGeneration, and Tesla are thrown out then the average PE multiples among the profitable cannabis and non-cannabis sector companies are comparable. Unfortunately, 50% of the providers of ancillary services lost money in 2020 as did 78.8% of the vertically integrated companies, while all 12 of the non-cannabis companies produced net profits after tax.

Investors who use the PE multiple as their sole valuation metric are likely to avoid buying cannabis company stocks, sine an overwhelming majority of cannabis companies are losing money and cannot produce a PE ratio. Cannabis companies must start earning a profit to capture investor attention.

PEG Ratio Valuation Metric

A large PE ratio is not necessarily alarming. In fact, companies with rapid growth rates will most often have high PE ratios. A PEG ratio, which is calculated by dividing a company's PE ratio by its growth rate in after tax earnings per share, is frequently used to factor in the importance of growth. A PEG ratio below 1.0 is supposed to signify an attractive investment opportunity.

Exhibit 5.4 shows PEG ratios using a one-year compound annual growth rate (CAGR). Among the seven cannabis companies with PE ratios in Exhibit 5.3 only Trulieve lent itself to PEG ratio analysis.

Exhibit 5.3
Price Earnings (PE) Multiple: 2020

Companies	Symbol	Multiple
Body & Mind	BMMJ	9.2
Next Green Wave	NXGWF	14.9
Vext Science	VEXTF	41.8
Vibe Growth	VBSCF	53.3
MariMed	MMNFF	59.5
Trulieve	TCNNF	60.0
Green Thumb	GTBIF	348.6
Providers		
Scotts Miracle-Gro	SMG	35.0
Innovative Industrial Propertie	IIPR	58.0
GrowGeneration	GRWG	574.6
Growth		
Facebook	FB	26.7
Google	GOOG	29.4
Microsoft	MSFT	38.0
Apple	APPL	39.2
Amazon	AMZN	76.8
Tesla	TSLA	981.8
Consumer Package Goods		
Philip Morris USA	PM	15.6
Proctor & Gamble	PG	26.7
Pepsicola	PEP	28.3
Coca Cola	KO	30.0
Anheuser-Busch InBev	BUD	97.3
Kraft Heinz	KHC	116.6

PEG ratios could not be calculated for Body & Mind, Green Thumb, Next Green Wave, and Vibe Growth because they all had net losses after taxes in 2019. A PEG ratio could also not be calculated for Vext Science, because its one-year CAGR was a negative 24% due to its after tax per share income dropping in 2020 from 2019. Data for 2019 were not available for Item 9 Labs, therefore, a meaningful PEG analysis could not be done for it.

Trulieve reported net income of taxes per basic share of $0.55 in 2020, $0.48 in 2019, and $0.11 in 2018. Its compound annual growth rate (CAGR) for its latest year was therefore 14.6% and its CAGR for the past two years was 123.6%. These are grammatically different growth rates and applying the most recent one year, per share CAGR gives Trulieve a Trulieve a PEG ratio of 4.1 (60.0/14.6). If, however, the net income after taxes per share CAGR for the most recent two-year period is applied then Trulieve's PEG ratio at the end of 2020 would have been an attractive PEG ratio of 0.49.

Exhibit 5.4
PEG Multiple: 2020

Companies	Symbol	PE Multiple	1 Year CAGR	PEG Ratio
Trulieve	TCNNF	60.0	14.6	4.11
Innovative Industrial Properties	IIPR	58.0	61.1	0.95
Growth				
Facebook	FB	26.7	57.7	0.46
Amazon	AMZN	76.8	81.8	0.94
Google	GOOG	29.4	19.3	1.52
Microsoft	MSFT	38.0	13.9	2.73
Apple	APPL	39.2	10.7	3.66
Consumer Package Goods				
Philip Morris USA	PM	15.6	11.9	1.31
Proctor & Gamble	PG	26.7	17.0	1.57
Coca Cola	KO	30.0	9.2	3.26

In order to shed further light on Trulieve's PEG ratio, its net income after taxes per share for its most recent quarter was examined. It showed that Trulieve reported per share net income after taxes of $0.25 for its first quarter of 2021, which ended March 31, 2021, which was 19% above its comparable March 31, 2020 quarter.

On March 31, 2021 Trulieve's stock closed at $45.50. Annualizing its March 31, 2021 quarterly earnings per share of $0.25 provides a PE ratio of 45.5 (45.5/1) and a PEG ratio of 2.39 (45/19).

A PEG ratio could only be calculated for one provider of ancillary products and services, since Scotts Miracle-Gro and Grow Generation experienced declines in their after-tax earnings per share in 2020. Innovative Industrial Properties reported its earning per share after taxes increased by 61.1% in 2020; therefore, it was able to produce an attractive PEG ratio of 0.95.

Among the growth and CPG companies, Tesla, Anheuser Busch InBev, Kraft, and Pepsicola were unable to grow their after-tax earnings per share in 2020. As a result, PEG ratios could not be calculated for them.

An examination of Exhibit 5.4 shows, based on only using the PEG ratio, Facebook offered the best value at the end of 2020 since it had the lowest ratio at 0.46. Another growth stock, Amazon, placed second with a PEG ratio of 0.94. Those two were then followed by Philip Morris at 1.31x, Google at 1.52x, Proctor & Gamble at 1.57x, Microsoft at 2.73x, Coca Cola at 3.26x, and Apple at 3.66x.

Fixation on Growth

Sadly, cannabis company CEOs along with their investment bankers and investor relations machines have convinced numerous investors that revenue growth is the magic elixir that will deliver unimaginable rewards. They tell people they are following the same path that was laid out so successfully by Jeff Bezos at Amazon who ignored profits and focused on growth.

Cannabis company stakeholders who are echoing the Amazon analogy are hallucinating perhaps on their own products. They seem to forget that Amazon has this thing called Amazon Prime which brings in billions in cash flow thereby reducing its need for external funding to almost nothing. In the minds of today's cannabis company stakeholders growth cures everything and that is delusional. Once a CEO starts comparing their cannabis company and strategy to that of Amazon and Jeff Bezos investors need to sell that company's shares as soon as possible.

The fixation on growth is probably the leading cause of cannabis companies reporting negative free cash flow and bleeding red ink. They ignorantly believe that size alone will enable them to reap rich rewards as shareholders bid up the price of their shares on growth alone. Most of them do not even distinguish between organic growth and growth originating from acquisitions. Hopefully this book will help to dispel the growth myth.

The extant literature is filled with projections on the growth in legal marijuana sales and what is referred to as the total addressable market (TAM). The nation's TAM is simply the sum of state TAMs. Once a U.S. MSO enters a new state its leaders are quick to point out the TAM of the state and by inference extrapolate that to the likely sales of their company. They invariably do this charade even though laws in that particular state limit them to owning only a handful of dispensaries.

Investors in cannabis stocks are especially conditioned to focus on growth. From their earliest purchase of a cannabis stock they have clung to the growth mantra. They are continually reminded by company spokespersons, financial publications, and security analysts about the growth a company is experiencing in sales and Adjusted EBITDA, because they are about the only positive numbers that can be reported.

The fact is that most of the growth is bought at the expense of shareholders. The correlation between revenue growth at cannabis companies and increases in the number of shares outstanding is near perfect. If you owned shares in a company that had $100 million in sales, and the CEO of that company bought another company that also had $100 million in sales, but paid for that new company by doubling the number of authorized shares and to give to the owners of the company they bought you would end up owning a smaller percentage of a bigger company.

Whether you would be better off would depend on if your earnings per share and cash flow per share increased. The chances are you would be worse off the CEO of your company would be way better off because his board of directors would likely reward the CEO for doubling the size of the company.

Time and time again, security analysts and investment bankers allow cannabis company CEOs and chief financial officers (CFOs) to focus on growth and Adjusted EBITDA on conference calls accompanying earnings releases without asking tough question such as:

What percentage of you revenue growth was attributable to same store sales? What percentage of your growth in sales is attributable to your recent acquisition? When do you expect to generate net income after taxes for tour shareholders? When do you expect to report a positive amount of cash provided from operations? Have you received any phone calls from the U.S. Government asking you to pay your back taxes?

The investment bankers are never going to ask those questions. Their very existence depends on business they get from the executives hosting the conference call.

Exhibit 5.5 shows the number of shares outstanding as reported by 34 vertically integrated cannabis companies on the final day of 2019 and 2020. The percentage increase in shares outstanding is shown for each company. Interestingly, Cansortium was the only company that reduced its shares outstanding.

As a group, these 34 companies increased the number of shares outstanding by 28.2%. The increase in number of shares was the result of share issuance in mergers and acquisitions along with issuance to simply raise necessary cash. The company that increased its outstanding shares by the greatest percentage was Stem Holdings, which increased its outstanding shares by 242.1%. Other companies with significant share issuance in 2020 were Red White & Bloom which increased its shares outstanding by 127.2%, Hollister Bioscience 120.6%, MedMen 98.0%, Ayr Wellness by 94.8%, Lowell Farms 75.4%, Jushi Holdings 64.8%, Plus Products 45.4%, and Curaleaf 41.2%.

If you as a shareholder of Ayr Wellness did not increase the number of shares you owned by 94.8% in 2020 then your percentage ownership of the company declined by that percentage. As long as Ayr Wellness continues to lose money you might find that acceptable. But if it turns the corner and starts making a profit you might be surprised by the fact that your shares of stock do not increase by the percentage you hoped for, and a major reason would be because your ownership position was diluted.

The extent to which some companies increase the number of potential shares outstanding is sometimes striking. Nowhere is that more apparent than with SPACs and Ayr Wellness is a prime example of a company that might make the old trailhands at the Kansas City stockyards blush.

As mentioned in Chapter 4, Ayr Wellness began its corporate life as a thinly capitalized SPAC raising only C$125 million in December 2017 with the issuance of 12.5 million shares at C$10 per share. In May 2019, eighteen months after its share issuance, it closed its qualifying transaction and emerged as a cannabis company and began to tout its expertise. Being relatively cash short, Ayr Wellness had to issue some stock; and, by the end of 2019 it had 14,824,485 million Subordinate, Restricted, Limited Voting shares issued and outstanding.

It continued to issue a significant amount of such stock and by the end of 2020 its Subordinate, Restricted, Limited Voting shares outstanding totaled 27,620,071 million, representing an increase of 94.8%.

Ayr Wellness stepped up its share issuance in early 2021 and on March 31, 2021 it reported it had 47,128,925 million Subordinate, Restricted, Limited Voting shares issued and outstanding. In a span of 15 months, it had increased the number of its Subordinate, Restricted, Limited Voting shares outstanding by an astonishing 217.9%.

Like most other cannabis companies the amount of subordinate shares is below the number of fully diluted shares. As previously mentioned, the number of fully diluted shares outstanding is a critical number used to ascertain the amount of cash flow and net income to which an investor is entitled. It therefore needs to be precise, because it plays a major role is figuring out the valuation multiples at which shares trade.

A deep dive into Ayr Wellness SEDAR and CSE filings showed that on March 31, 2021 it had 3,696,486 Multiple Voting Shares (MVS) and 6,347,565 Exchangeable Shares convertible into Subordinate shares on a one-to-one basis at no cost to the owner.

Additionally, Ayr had 10,022,106 in-the-money (ITM) warrants exercisable at C$11.50, at a time its AYRWF closing price was $30.12. It also had 45,471 rights convertible into 456 Subordinate shares. When Ayr acquired Liberty Health Sciences it assumed $4,325,000 in Liberty Health convertible debentures (convertible at C$0.83) and about 3,000,000 in exercisable, ITM options. On March 31, 2021 only $2,862,500 of the debentures remained outstanding. The remaining debentures and the inherited options could cause the issuance of about those 225,000 Ayr Subordinate shares. Additionally, Ayr has issued 5,261,150 Restricted Stock Units (RSUs) to top executives entitling them receive an equal number of Subordinate shares without any cost.

If all the enumerated additional shares are added, Ayr would possibly have to issue an additional 25,552,763 Subordinate, Restricted, Limited Voting shares. Those shares need to be added to the number of Subordinate shares outstanding on March 31, 2021 to arrive at the total number of diluted shares. When that is done, the number of diluted Ayr Subordinated shares outstanding reaches 72,681,688.

Exhibit 5.5
Cannabis Company Shares Outstanding: 2019 and 2020

Company	Symbol	Shares Outstanding 2019	Shares Outstanding 2020	Increase	Total revenue 2019	Total revenue 2020	Increase
Curaleaf	CURLF	470,085,071	663,801,845	41.2%	221,018,000	626,637,000	183.5%
Green Thumb	GTBIF	206,563,864	213,345,221	3.3%	216,432,605	556,572,889	157.2%
Trulieve	TCNNF	110,346,346	119,573,998	8.4%	252,819,000	521,533,000	106.3%
Cresco Labs	CRLBF	274,209,000	384,801,220	40.3%	128,534,000	476,251,000	270.5%
Terrascend	TRSSF	180,870,422	209,692,379	15.9%	65,283,077	152,552,308	133.7%
Columbia Care	CCHWF	216,529,181	276,511,831	27.7%	128,534,000	179,503,000	39.7%
Harvest Health	HRVSF	289,125,527	405,755,458	40.3%	65,283,077	231,460,000	254.5%
Chalice Brands Ltd	CHALF	854,384,638	961,742,734	12.6%	15,754,607	21,909,156	39.1%
Planet 13	PLNHF	137,660,559	181,806,190	32.1%	63,595,036	70,491,280	10.8%
Ayr Wellness	AYRWF	14,824,485	28,873,641	94.8%	75,195,556	155,114,454	106.3%
Jushi Holdings	JUSHF	91,842,638	151,386,081	64.8%	10,229,000	80,772,000	689.6%
4Front Ventures	FFNTF	531,522,819	538,851,252	1.4%	19,032,000	57,635,000	202.8%
Acreage Holdings	ACRHF	90,646,000	101,250,000	11.7%	74,109,000	114,545,000	54.6%
Goodness Holdings	GDNSF	85,218,311	113,016,459	32.6%	29,956,172	49,211,329	64.3%
Item 9 Labs	INLB	63,724,905	75,261,084	18.1%	6,466,816	9,628,441	48.9%
Gage Growth	GAEGF	105,622,799	131,649,944	24.6%	1,925,133	39,880,407	1971.6%
MariMed	MRMD	228,408,024	314,418,812	37.7%	45,604,644	50,895,151	11.6%
Tilt Holdings	TLLTF	362,279,572	367,182,673	1.4%	146,935,000	158,409,000	7.8%
MedMen	MMNFF	258,698,255	512,315,834	98.0%	138,443,309	142,778,033	3.1%
Cansortium	CNTMF	193,495,462	187,915,751	-2.9%	28,511,000	52,388,000	83.7%
Red White & Bloom	RWBYF	84,211,770	191,317,226	127.2%	1,671,499	23,338,528	1296.3%
C21 Investments	CXXIF	89,388,739	117,057,860	31.0%	37,705,095	36,127,286	-4.2%
Next Green Wave	NXGWF	164,670,189	177,394,283	7.7%	285,953	12,627,677	4316.0%
Stem Holdings	STMH	52,754,211	180,475,239	242.1%	2,451,000	13,974,000	470.1%
Harborside	HBORF	42,097,704	44,445,208	5.6%	49,452,539	59,953,717	21.2%
Medicine Man	SHWZ	39,952,628	42,601,773	6.6%	12,400,955	24,000,852	93.5%
Lowell Farms	LOWLF	32,844,000	57,617,000	75.4%	37,045,000	42,618,000	15.0%
Slang Worldwide	SLGWF	257,729,502	321,650,058	24.8%	22,483,950	20,630,444	-8.2%
Vibe Growth	VBSCF	77,577,212	82,613,028	6.5%	12,600,159	24,240,862	92.4%
Vext Science	VEXTF	84,353,326	115,153,491	36.5%	22,322,568	25,193,958	12.9%
Hollister Bio	HSTRF	108,777,373	239,978,113	120.6%	1,012,192	30,576,267	2920.8%
Body & Mind	BMMJ	101,853,217	108,377,778	6.4%	6,289,136	25,261,644	301.7%
iAnthus Capital	ITHUF	171,643,192	171,718,192	0.0%	78,382,000	151,669,000	93.5%
Plus Products	PLPRF	33,745,986	49,066,222	45.4%	13,850,351	15,863,446	14.5%

The difference between the reported number of Subordinate shares and the number of fully diluted Subordinate shares is a stunning 54.2%. This is of major significance to shareholders, because the percentage of profits to which a shareholder is entitled is equal to the number of shares they own divided by the total number of "fully diluted" shares outstanding. For example, if you owned half of all the Ayr Subordinate shares outstanding on March 31, 2021, you would own only about 32.4% of the company.

When Liberty Health Sciences announced on December 22, 2020 that it had signed a definitive agreement to be acquired by Ayr its new release stated: "Liberty shareholders are expected to hold approximately 20% ownership in the pro forma entity (on a fully-diluted in-the-money basis) …inclusive of shares to be issued relating to previously disclosed Ayr acquisitions in Pennsylvania and Arizona and recently announced acquisition in New Jersey and is calculated on a fully-diluted in-the-money basis using the treasury stock method." For what it's worth, Liberty Health shareholders received 12,670,958 shares of Ayr on February 26, 2021; and, those shares represented about 17.4% ownership of Ayr Wellness.

Accretion and Dilution

Despite the alarming increase in the number of shares outstanding, cannabis CEOs continue to announce that their current acquisition is immediately accretive. That lie is designed to comfort existing shareholders and make them feel as if they are going to benefit. These CEOs are invariably referring to the fact that total revenue and their beloved Adjusted EBITDA or some other favored metric are going to increase. In their minds, increases in those items are accretive. That is simply not true!

As mentioned earlier, companies report earnings after taxes per share on the basis of actual shares outstanding and on the basis of diluted shares outstanding. A shareholder's claim on after tax earnings is equal to their percentage ownership of the company, which is represented by the number of shares they own relative to the total number of shares outstanding. A shareholder's claim in liquidation after settlement of debts equals their percentage share ownership.

If a merger or acquisition occurs and you as a shareholder experience reduced earnings per share or increased loss per share, you are worse off and the transaction is dilutive not accretive. Cannabis company CEOs who claim their M&A transactions are immediately accretive are living in a fantasy world. If what they say is true then the office supply stores near cannabis company headquarters wouldn't have to continually stock red ink!

The following is a vivid illustration of the extent to which cannabis companies are bastardizing the financial meaning of accretion. It is a statement taken directly from a June 15, 2021 Columbia Care press release announcing the signing of a definitive agreement to acquire Medicine Man. The second bullet point in the press release states the transaction is: "Immediately accretive to Columbia Care's gross margin, Adjusted EBITDA, and free cash flow." Similar statements abound in press releases of other cannabis companies. This particular one just happened to be handy at the time this section was being written. At the very minimum, statements such as the one cited above are misleading.

Exhibit 5.6 presents comparable data on shares outstanding at the six companies which provide of ancillary products and services, the six growth companies, and the six consumer package goods companies. Four of the providers significantly increased the number of their shares outstanding.

Innovative Industrial Properties had the largest percentage increase in shares outstanding at 89.4%; however, that increase was dwarfed by its 294% increase in after tax income. Similarly, GrowGeneration increased its shares outstanding by 37.7%, but it increased after tax earnings by 284%. Greenlane, Hydrofarm, and KushCo all had net losses after taxes in 2020, so their share issuance did not help their shareholders.

The most telling thing about Exhibit 5.6 is it shows that growth companies and consumer package goods companies are not issuing additional shares. If anything, they are following Warren Buffet's advice and reducing the number of shares they have outstanding. As noted in Exhibit 5.6, Apple, Facebook, Google, and Microsoft all decreased their outstanding shares in 2020 even though they enjoyed significant growth. Among the consumer packaged goods companies, Kraft, Pepsicola, and Proctor and Gamble decreased their outstanding shares.

There are only two legitimate ways to increase cash flow per share at a company. One way is to simply increase the amount of cash provided by operations; the other way is to decrease the number of shares outstanding. As of the end of 2020, cannabis companies (with very few exceptions) were doing neither. In fact, they were doing it backwards by increasing the negative cash provided by operations and by sharply increasing the number of shares outstanding.

Exhibit 5.6
Shares Outstanding: 2019 and 2020

Company	Symbol	2019	2020	Increase
GrowGeneration	GRWG	228,408,024	314,418,812	37.7%
Greenlane Holdings	GNLN	93,578,000	92,852,000	-0.8%
Hydrofarm Holdings	HYFM	20,688,439	33,499,953	61.9%
Innovative Industrial	IIPR	12,637,000	23,937,000	89.4%
KushCo Holdings	KSHB	119,118,000	158,763,000	33.3%
Scotts Miracle-Gro	SMG	68,100,000	68,100,000	0.0%
Growth				
Amazon	AMZN	498,000,000	503,000,000	1.0%
Apple	APPL	17,772,944,000	16,976,763,000	-4.5%
Facebook	FB	2,852,000,000	2,849,000,000	-0.1%
Google	GOOG	688,335,000	675,222,000	-1.9%
Microsoft	MSFT	7,643,000,000	7,571,000,000	-0.9%
Tesla	TSLA	905,310,000	960,000,000	6.0%
Consumer Package Goods				
Anheuser-Busch InBev	BUD	1,959,379,000	1,972,249,000	0.7%
Coca Cola	KO	4,280,129,000	4,302,129,000	0.5%
Kraft Heinz	KHC	1,223,000,000	1,221,000,000	-0.2%
Pepsicola	PEP	1,391,000,000	1,380,000,000	-0.8%
Philip Morris USA	PM	1,555,895,000	1,557,374,000	0.1%
Proctor & Gamble	PG	2,504,751,000	2,479,700,000	-1.0%

It is also true that there are only two legitimate ways to increase after tax earnings per share at a company. One way is to simply increase the amount of net income after taxes by increasing revenue more than expenses; the other way is to decrease the number of shares outstanding. As of the end of 2020, cannabis companies were doing neither of these things either.

Book Value Valuation Metric

Old time investors long for the halcyon days when they could acquire company stock at book value. The fact is that very few publicly traded stocks of viable companies are available at book value. If they are available at book value then extra care should be exercised to ascertain why? Book value, also known as shareholders' equity, is important for a number of reasons.

It measures how much capital is available to weather a storm. A firm that has negative capital is de facto insolvent and a leading candidate for Chapter 7 bankruptcy. Interestingly, owners of cannabis companies that become insolvent may not be able to avail themselves of U.S. Federal Bankruptcy protections for two reasons. First, cannabis is a Schedule 1 Substance and illegal from a Federal point of view. Secondly, almost all the publicly held cannabis companies operating in the United States are incorporated in Canada. With that in mind, investors in cannabis companies that currently have negative equity or almost no equity might want to position themselves near an exit.

Exhibit 5.1 shows that Jushi Holdings multiple of book value could not be calculated for Jushi. The reason was that it reported negative shareholders' equity in its audited 2020 annual report amounting to $177,000.

Among the other companies, the one with the richest valuation based on book value alone was Plus Products. Its stock was selling at 520.5x book value per share and it was followed closely by Terrascend at 246.4x. Other companies with double digit metrics in descending order were Chalice Brands 87.7X, MariMed 17.9x, 4Front Ventures 11.6, and Item 9 Labs.

Companies whose stocks were selling below book value included iAnthus at 0.7x, MedMen at 0.4x, and Tilt Holdings at 0.4x. Each of those companies was experiencing serious problems at the time. In fact, on April 6, 2020 iAnthus announced it had defaulted on interest payments due on its 13.0% Senior Secured Debentures and 13.0% Unsecured Convertible Debentures that had been due on March 31, 2020. In the week prior to its announcement iAnthus traded as high as $0.60 per share and on the day of the announced default it traded as low as $0.16 and closed at $0.18.

MedMen had been troubled company for some time and that was reflected in its year end stock price of $0.13. It had once been a heavily touted cannabis stock which traded as high as about $8 in October 2018. Its marketing strategy was to open cannabis stores in exclusive locales like Rodeo Drive in Beverly Hills, California; Worth Avenue in Palm Beach, Florida; Fifth Avenue in New York City; and create a high-end brand. The bibliography in Appendix C includes very interesting articles about MedMen.

Tilt Holdings at the end of 2020 was continuing to suffer from its inglorious start. It went public in Canada toward the end of 2018, and in its first quarterly earnings report it announced a goodwill impairment charge of $500 million. Overcoming such a checkered past is not easy, so it is not surprising that Tilt's shares were trading at less than half book value.

The brief discussion of iAnthus, MedMen, and Tilt Holdings vividly illustrate the need to do more research when something seems out of order. A little research is well worth the effort and locating information has never been easier thanks to internet search engines.

The top five Canadian LPs stock prices as multiples of book value per share at the end of 2020 ranged from a low of 0.7x for Aurora Cannabis to a high of 3.5x for Tilray. Cronos and Aphria stocks both traded at 1.5x book values per share, while Canopy Growth stock traded at 2.8x.

Exhibit 5.7 shows the book value multiples for stocks of (1) providers of ancillary products and services to cannabis companies, (2) well know growth companies, and (3) consumer package goods companies. GrowGeneration stock carries a high multiple of book value at 39.9x as do Greenlane at 24.4x and Scotts Miracle-Gro at 19.3. Those multiples along with Apple at 34.5X, Tesla at 20.8, and Amazon at 17.5 are high compared with most vertically integrated cannabis companies and consumer package goods companies, whose stocks sold at single digit multiples of their book value per share.

Exhibit 5.7
Book Value Multiples

Companies	Symbol	Multiple
Providers		
KushCo Holdings	KSHB	1.0
Innovative Industrial	IIPR	2.6
Hydrofarm Holdings	HYFM	8.4
Scotts Miracle-Gro	SMG	19.3
Greenlane Holdings	GNLN	24.4
GrowGeneration	GRWG	39.9
Growth		
Google	GOOG	5.0
Facebook	FB	6.1
Microsoft	MSFT	9.3
Amazon	AMZN	17.5
Tesla	TSLA	20.8
Apple	APPL	34.5
Consumer Package Goods		
Kraft	KHC	0.5
Anheuser-Busch InBev	BUD	0.8
Pepsicola	PEP	3.5
Coca Cola	KO	3.7
Proctor & Gamble	PG	4.2
Philip Morris USA	PM	6.6

Tangible Book Value Valuation Metric

The risk of impairment charges is real as previously noted in the Tilt Holdings situation and in the $2+ billion impairment charges taken by Aurora Cannabis, which was discussed in Chapter 2. Shareholders of companies with large amounts of goodwill and intangible assets will always face the threat of impairment charges. At the time of an impairment charge, the damage that can be done to a stock price is proportional to the ratio of goodwill plus intangibles to shareholders' equity.

If the total of a company's goodwill and intangible assets equals only 5% of its shareholders' equity and all of it had to be charged-off the company would still be left with 95% of its equity. If, however, the total of a company's goodwill and intangible assets equals 100% of its shareholders' equity and all of it had to be charged-off, the very survival of that company would be in doubt. Even if 50% was charged-off the company would face serious problems and the stock price would likely be slammed lower.

Cannabis company balance sheets are loaded with goodwill and intangible assets. Shareholders of cannabis companies, therefore, are likely to face impairment charges in the future as acquisitions fail to deliver sufficient after-tax earnings to justify existing goodwill and as cannabis licenses become more readily available.

Exhibit 5.1 shows the seriousness of the situation. It reveals that 14 (40%) of the 35 cannabis companies had goodwill and intangible assets that exceeded their shareholders' equity at the end of 2020. That situation precluded calculating a tangible book value metric, so "NM" was entered in Exhibit 5.1.

A close inspection of the raw data showed the company whose goodwill and intangible assets exceeded their shareholders equity by the greatest percentage was Terrascend. At the end of 2020 it reported $100,517,000 in goodwill, $165,705,000 in intangible assets, and shareholders' equity of $11,117,000. Its goodwill and intangible assets were, therefore, 23.9x its shareholders equity. As such, a write-off or impairment charge of as little as 4.2% of goodwill and intangibles would make Terrascend insolvent in that its liabilities would exceed its assets and its shareholders equity would be negative.

The above analysis strongly suggested that Terrascend needed to bolster its capital position at the end of 2020. It is not surprising that the Terrascend financial filing for March 31, 2021 revealed it increased its shareholders' equity by issuing about $200 million in new stock during the first quarter of 2021. As a result of the capital injection, its ratio of goodwill + intangibles to shareholders equity dropped to a still high 96.5%.

Other companies whose goodwill + intangible assets equaled or exceeded their shareholders' equity at the end of 2020 in descending order were Harborside at 3.9x, Cansortium 3.5x, iAnthus 3.1x, AyrWellness 2.3x, 21 Investments 1.6x, Medicine Man1.3, Stem 1.2x, 4Front 1.2x, Slang 1.1x, Harvest 1.0x, and MedMen 1.0x. Shareholders of all companies with loads of goodwill and intangible assets are at much greater risk of sudden impairment charges as the cannabis landscape changes.

Among the five largest cannabis companies, Trulieve traded at the smallest multiple of its tangible book value at 13.3x. Curaleaf's comparable multiple was 73.1x.

The degree to which cannabis companies have loaded their balance sheets with goodwill and intangible assets is alarming. There are few if any industries where the participants have such a high percentage of assets in these two categories and this gives rise to the very significant difference between book value and tangible book value observed among cannabis companies.

Significant differences between these two measures of book value exist, because most cannabis companies were initially formed by rolling up existing limited liability entities at prices well above book value. Also, most of the mergers and acquisitions have involved transactions well above book value. Most cannabis companies also continue to add to their accumulated deficits by losing money thereby decreasing their book value. Any investor who ignores the tangible book value of cannabis companies is making a big mistake.

The top five Canada LP stocks traded at widely different multiples of tangible equity capital at the end of 2020. Cronos and Aurora Cannabis tangible equity multiples were both 1.7, followed by Canopy Growth at 4.9x, then Aphria at 23.7x and Tilray at 63.7x. That variability mirrors the variability observable among the cannabis companies shown in Exhibit 5.1.

Recent mergers and acquisitions suggest that the providers of ancillary products and services are also increasing the tangible book value multiples of their stock. At the end of its fiscal 2020, Scotts Miracle-Gro actually had negative tangible equity capital of $520.4 million. It had intangible assets of $679.2 million, goodwill of $544.1 million and only $702.9 million in shareholders' equity. Greenlane had a tangible equity multiple of 63x and the acquisitive GrowGeneration's stock sold at 54.4x its tangible equity.

Adjusted Operating Income Valuation Metric

Chapter 2 devoted considerable attention to gross profit margins, operating expenses, and net operating income of fully integrated cannabis companies. Exhibit 5.1 brings it down to the shareholder level, since it shows a company's stock price as a multiple of adjusted net operating income, which excludes the impact of biologicals so IFRS and GAAP reporting results would be comparable.

Unfortunately, Exhibit 5.1 shows that only nine (25.7%) of the 35 companies had positive adjusted net operating income. Of those nine, the company whose stock was trading at the lowest multiple of adjusted net operating income per share was Medicine Man which had a 14.6x multiple.

It was followed in ascending order by Trulieve at 17.3x, Vibe Growth at 23.2x, Next Green Wave at 24.0x, MariMed at 32.2x, Vext Science at 34.0x, Green Thumb at 49.3x, Terrascend at 120.4x, and Ayr Wellness at 523.1x.

Among the nine largest cannabis companies only two had positive adjusted net operating income. Trulieve's stock traded at 17.3x net operating income per share, while Green Thumb traded at 49.3x.

The fact that so few fully integrated companies are able to generate net operating income is not a healthy. It also does not suggest that the cannabis business is a bird's nest on the ground.

Adjusted EBITDA Valuation Metric

Given the cannabis sector's inability to produce free cash flow from operations along with after tax profits, it is not surprising that cannabis companies and their investment bankers have dreamt up another performance metric. As profits and free cash flow failed to materialize, cannabis companies and investment bankers with increasing frequency started touting Adjusted EBITDA as the metric investors needed to look at.

Chapter 3 addressed numerous issues that surround the use of the "adjusted IBITDA valuation metric and seriously questioned the legitimacy of this Non-IFRS, Non-GAAP measure. Exhibit 5.1 presents a company's share price as a multiple of its Adjusted EBITDA per share. Other things being equal, fans of Adjusted EBITDA would prefer to buy stocks trading at the lowest multiple of Adjusted EBITDA.

Exhibit 5.1 shows that 14 cannabis companies were unable to produce positive Adjusted EBITDA for the year ended 2020. Perhaps these 14 companies were unaware of the 44 items or ingredients (Exhibit 2.4) that were used by other publicly held cannabis companies to create a more palatable number. The companies able to generate positive Adjusted EBITDA are probably laughing at those less creative than themselves.

Of those that did have positive metrics, Tilt's stock price was selling at the lowest multiple of Adjusted EBITDA per share. Its multiple was 6.3x and it was followed in ascending order by MariMed at 8.1x, Vest Science at 13.0x, Vibe Growth at 13.1, Cansortium at 14.1, Ayr Wellness at 14.7x, Next Green Wave at 14.9x, Trulieve at 15.1x, Body & Mind at 15.9, and C21 Investments at 16.9. All the others had multiples of above 29x.

Among the five largest cannabis companies, Trulieve's stock was selling at the lowest multiple of Adjusted EBITDA 15.1x. Curaleaf had the highest of the top 5 at 55.1x.

Amazingly, the five large Canadian LPs, who invented/concocted/and basically cooked up "Adjusted EBITDA" as the Holy Grail of cannabis company valuation were unable to report positive figures for fiscal 2020.

Total Revenue Valuation Metric

The final valuation metric used to determine the relative valuation of a stock is total revenue. The nice thing about this measure is that every cannabis company in Exhibit 5.1 had revenue. An earlier version of Exhibit 5.1 included Zynerba Pharmaceuticals, which at one time was a stock holding of the MSOS ETF; however, once data started to be uploaded onto spreadsheets it was discovered Zynerba had no revenue in 2019 or 2020.

The problem is that all revenue is not the same. For example, total revenue might include wholesale as well as retail sales. Some revenue might also be revenue from royalties and rent. Profit percentages obviously differ greatly based on the source of revenue.

It is certainly better, however, to calculate revenue per share and express a stock price as a multiple of that than it is to just look at total revenue for an entire company. That is especially true for cannabis companies that have been issuers of large amounts of stock.

Exhibit 5.1 shows that if iAnthus, MedMen, and Tilt Holdings are excluded, then the cheapest stock is Harborside at 1.4x revenue. It is followed by Lowell Farms at 1.5x, Hollister Bio and Plus Products at 1.6x, Body & Mind at 1.7x, Medicine Man at 2.6x, Acreage Holdings at 2.7x, MariMed and Cansortium at 2.8x, and Goodness Holdings at 3.4.

Among the five largest cannabis companies their stocks traded between Trulieve's 7.4x revenue to Curaleaf's 12.7x. The stock of Chalice Brands traded at the highest multiple which was 21.9x revenue.

The five large Canada LPs had stock prices that ranged from a low multiple of 3.6x revenue at Aphria to a high of 53.5x at Cronos. Aurora Cannabis traded at 5.4x revenue per share, Tilray at 6.2x, and Canopy growth at 22.0x.

The stock prices of the providers of ancillary products and services, and those of well-known growth and consumer package companies are expressed as multiples of per share revenue and shown in Exhibit 5.8. Based on this metric, KushCo offered the best value among the providers since its stock was selling at only 1.1x revenue per share; Amazon offered the best value among growth companies at 4.2x; and Kraft Heinz offered the best value among consumer package goods companies. The worst value in each company category was the provider GrowGeneration which had a stock price equal to 65.4x revenue per share; the growth company Tesla at 21.5x revenue; and Coca Cola at 7.0x revenue.

Exhibit 5.8
Revenue Multiples

Companies	Symbol	Multiple
Providers		
KushCo Holdings	KSHB	1.1
Greenlane Holdings	GNLN	2.7
Scotts Miracle-Gro	SMG	3.3
Hydrofarm Holdings	HYFM	5.1
Innovative Industrial	IIPR	18.2
GrowGeneration	GRWG	65.4
Growth		
Amazon	AMZN	4.2
Google	GOOG	6.5
Apple	APPL	8.2
Facebook	FB	9.1
Microsoft	MSFT	11.8
Tesla	TSLA	21.5
Consumer Package Goods		
Kraft Heinz	KHC	1.6
Anheuser-Busch InBev	BUD	2.9
Pepsicola	PEP	2.9
Philip Morris USA	PM	4.4
Proctor & Gamble	PG	4.8
Coca Cola	KO	7.0

A comparison of all companies based on the stock price as a multiple of per share revenue suggests that larger cannabis company stocks are very richly valued relative to consumer package goods companies and richly valued relative to well know growth companies. Once a company stock price to revenue per share multiple reaches double digit levels an investor needs to be concerned about possible overvaluation. It is easy to see why GrowGeneration has captured the attention of short sellers.

Large Canadian LP Stock Valuation Metrics

Although data for the five largest Canadian LPs was included throughout this chapter, Exhibit 5.9 puts all the valuation metrics in one easily accessible spot. It is unfortunate that most of the valuation metrics could not be calculated because of losses and negative cash flows.

A comparison of Exhibit 5.9 with 5.1 indicates that large Canadian LP stocks sell at lower multiples of book value than their large counterparts in the United States. Exhibit 5.3 also shows that Aphria and Tilray had significantly more goodwill and intangible assets on their balance sheets than their Canadian peers. Of course, this snapshot of Aurora Cannabis was taken shortly after it cleaned up its balance sheet by charging off $2.8 billion.

Exhibit 5.9
Valuation Metrics for Top 5 Canadian Licensed Producers for 2020

		Share Price as Multiple of Per Share Amounts of						
Company	Symbol	Oper Cash Flow	NIAT	Book Value	Tangible Book Value	Adj Oper Income	Adj EBITDA	Total Rev
Canopy Growth	CGC	NM	NM	2.8	4.9	NM	NM	22.0
Cronos	CRON	NM	NM	1.5	1.7	NM	NM	53.5
Aurora Cannabis	ACB	NM	NM	0.7	1.7	NM	NM	5.4
Aphria	APHA	NM	NM	1.5	23.7	NM	NM	3.6
Tilray	TLRY	NM	NM	3.5	63.7	NM	NM	6.2

The sad thing is that these cannabis companies have been in business for several years and still cannot produce profits and positive cash flow. If they are the canaries the coal mine, it does not augur well for cannabis company shareholders.

Providers of Ancillary Products and Services Valuation Metrics

Stock valuation metrics for the providers of ancillary products and services to those who cultivate, process, and distribute cannabis products are not a homogeneous group of companies that can be easily compared with each other. They have been discussed at various points in this chapter, however, it seems appropriate their valuation metrics be presented in one exhibit. Exhibit 5.10 shows valuation metrics for these providers.

Innovative Industrial Properties stands out for its success. As a REIT that must payout 90% of its income annually to avoid taxation at the corporate level, its yield of 4.8% dwarfs the dividend yield of any other provider as well as the nonexistent yield on vertically integrated companies. Its incredible performance had already been discussed in Chapter 4 and nothing much can be added.

The Scotts Miracle-Gro Company cannot be compared to the margins of Hydrofarm Holdings. Despite these limitations, metrics shown for providers of ancillary products and services to cannabis companies shed important light on relative valuations within the cannabis sector as well as outside the sector.

Innovative Industrial clearly stands out from the other companies in that it had positive operating cash flow, was profitable, and paid an attractive 4.80% dividend. It had a high PE ratio but an attractive PEG ratio of 0.95 once its earnings per share growth rate of 61.1% was divided into its PE of 58.0.

By comparison, GrowGeneration which was been another huge Wall Street success story in 2020 was trading at an astronomical PE of 574.6. With a growth rate of 142.2% GrowGeneration had a relatively high PEG ratio of 4.04.

Exhibit 5.10
Valuation Metrics for Providers of Ancillary Products/Services for 2020

Company	Symbol	Oper Cash Flow	NIAT PE Ratio	Growth Rate NIAT	PEG Ratio	Book Value	Total Rev	Dividend Yield
Innovative Industrial	IIPR	43.6	58.0	61.10%	0.95	3.5	18.2	4.80%
Scotts Miracle-Gro	SMG	24.3	35.0	-16.2%	NM	8.4	3.3	2.50%
GrowGeneration	GRWG	NM	574.6	142.2%	4.04	39.9	65.4	NA
Jazz Pharmaceuticals	JAZZ	11.0	40.4	-54.2%	NM	2.6	4.1	NA
Hydrofarm Holdings	HYFM	NM	NM	NM	NM	8.4	5.1	NA
Greenlane Holdings	GNLN	NM	NM	NM	NM	24.4	2.7	NA
KushCo Holdings	KSHB	NM	NM	NM	NM	1.0	1.1	NA

Frankly, Hydrofarm, Greenlane, and KushCo seem to have caught the financial disease that afflicts the vertically integrated cannabis companies. Like their customers they show no evidence of producing positive cash flow from operations or after-tax profits.

Summary

At the end of 2020 a majority of the cannabis companies engaged in cultivation, processing, and distribution along with the providers of products and services to them were unable to generate positive cash flow from operations or net income after taxes. This observation is true for the top Canadian cannabis companies and those in the United States.

Despite those failures they continued to implement growth strategies requiring massive amounts of external funds. In that process, they have improperly conveyed their actions are accretive while issuing large amounts of common shares and other types of convertible securities that actually dilute existing shareholders.

This chapter has shown that the risk to shareholders from possible goodwill and intangible write-offs (impairments) is large and growing. That risk will rise or fall based on the ability of individual companies to generate net income after taxes and positive cash from operations excluding non-payment of taxes in 2021 and 2022.

CHAPTER 6

EPILOGUE

Many changes are certain to occur from the time this book is printed until the time you read it. Pending mergers and acquisitions are likely to be consummated including Trulieve's acquisition of Harvest Health, Ceres' merging with Parallel, Columbia Care's acquisition of Medicine Man, KushCo's merger with Greenlane, and many more. These transactions will certainly be significant for shareholders in companies involved in these transactions; however, they will not have a transformative impact on the U.S. cannabis industry.

While some companies discussed in this book will disappear as separate public entities others will take their place as existing private cannabis companies get rolled up and taken public in IPOs. Investors will continue to be challenged to pick winning cannabis stocks and avoiding calamities like iAnthus.

The most important changes likely to face cannabis investors between the time you read this book and it gets printed will be legislative in origin. More states will certainly liberalize their laws thereby allowing greater access to cannabis. At the same time states will liberalize the form in which cannabis can be consumed. States that now prohibit smokable marijuana and the sale of edibles will likely alter their exclusions. States will also expand the number of licenses they issue as they realize how much more revenue could be brought into state revenue streams.

While changes at the state level are meaningful, they are not likely to have a significant impact on a cannabis-companies outside a given state. A major liberalization of license issuance could, however, have a deleterious impact on the financial statements of companies which acquired licenses at significantly higher prices. A surge in issuance could lead to write-offs or impairment charges that could be painful for some companies.

Change at the Federal level, should it occur, is likely to have a profound impact on cannabis companies. Descheduling cannabis from its current listing as a Schedule 1 drug like heroin and opium would allow cannabis companies to have bank accounts, accept credit cards, uplist their stocks onto the NYSE and NASDAQ exchanges, allow major brokerage firms and other institutions to buy and sell cannabis stocks, and effectively do away with IRC Section 280E.

The removal of IRC Section 280E would likely have the greatest immediate impact, since it would remove the burdensome non-deductibility of most cannabis company expenses. It would provide an immediate benefit to shareholders of vertically integrated cannabis companies operating in the United States. Their after-tax earnings and free cash flow per share would both immediately increase which should translate to high prices for those securities.

Some indication of what would happen to cannabis stocks was clearly shown in euphoria that spread following the Georgia Senate runoffs. When it became known that Democrats had won both seats, the prices of cannabis stocks surged by about 50 percent and volume exploded higher. That euphoria lasted about a week, and then market participants realized Federal legislation liberalizing cannabis laws was not a done deal.

Investors who believe commercial banks are anxious to lend to cannabis companies are bound to be severely disappointed. As shown in this book, there are very few vertically integrated cannabis companies or providers of ancillary products and services to those companies that are profitable or generating free cash flow. The likelihood is that any loan made to such companies will be immediately classified by bank examiners as either substandard, doubtful, or loss. Commercial lenders who chose to make such loans could be jeopardizing their careers.

While the legislative landscape will likely change by the time you read this book, the methodological approach to determining the value of one cannabis company relative to another will not change. Furthermore, the methodological approach enunciated in this book to determine the relative value of cannabis stocks to stocks in other sectors will not change. The valuation metrics presented in this book will be as relevant 100 years from now in 2121 as they were 100 years ago in 1921. New metrics will come and go, but they will not stand the test of time.

The fact is there are hundreds of industries and thousands of stocks competing for your investment attention and dollars. At the present time, cannabis companies have a serious problem competing for investment dollars because they have not yet demonstrated an ability to generate consistent and growing net income after taxes and free cash flow on a per share basis.

To meet their needs for cash cannabis companies have issued massive amounts of stock that has seriously diluted existing shareholders. They have also been forced to issue debt and enter into long-term leases containing astronomical interest rates. These deleterious trends must end.

The fact that U.S. cannabis stocks trade on the over-the-counter (OTC) and the Canadian Securities Exchange (CSE) is a huge negative. These exchanges have well deserved reputations for separating unsophisticated investors from their money and are sometimes referred to as the badlands.

It is not surprising that a number of brokerage firms will not buy or sell securities on the OTC and CSE exchanges. Furthermore, options on cannabis stocks traded on those exchanges are not available and neither is margin credit. The spreads between bid and ask prices are generally large and volume is low, so any trade you enter better be a limit order. In a limit order to buy, you agree to buy a specific number of shares at or below a stipulated price. In a limit order to sell, you agree to sell a specific number of shares at or above a stipulated price. It is difficult to conjure up anything to say about buying and selling stocks on the OTC and the CSE exchanges except caveat emptor.

Unfortunately, current regulations prevent U.S. cannabis companies that "touch the plant" from listing on the NYSE and NASDAQ. For example, Greenrose Acquisition Corporation, a SPAC, had to move from NASDAQ to OTC, when it decided to do its qualifying transaction with a company that cultivates, processes, and distributes cannabis.

Investors continually try to determine the best sectors in which to invest; and, within those sectors, investors try to ascertain which company's stock offers the best relative value. The fact is that investors can acquire thousands of stocks in hundreds of industries without encountering any transactions costs thanks to the existence of free trading.

Investors in cannabis stocks need to understand that diversification does not mean simply owning a portfolio of cannabis stocks or a cannabis ETF. It means owning a portfolio of stocks of companies that are in many different industries. Unfortunately, cannabis stock investors seem to have a penchant for having highly concentrated portfolios composed of stocks of companies in which they have intensely positive feelings.

The depth of cannabis company stockholder loyalty is conveyed in Tweets on Twitter, conversations on Yahoo Finance message boards, Facebook posts, Reddit, and other social media sites. No amount of factual information seems to shake the faith of a person who has loaded their boat with the stock of a particular cannabis company or ETF they have decided will soar in price.

Hopefully, the information provided in this book will enable you to make more informed decisions about what cannabis stocks you should buy.

July 31, 2021

APPENDIX A

PUBLICLY HELD CANNABIS COMPANIES

The following is an alphabetical listing and brief profile of every publicly held cannabis company mentioned in this book. Profiles of every company were obtained either from their own latest press releases or profiles published on Yahoo Finance. Those profiles were edited to delete comments that were deemed to be more promotional than factual. For example, one company in a press release stated, "it was led by an industry-leading management team," and that statement was deleted from its profile.

The stock trading symbol of every company is presented. Most trade on the over the counter "OTC" market in the United States and on the Canadian Securities Exchange "CSE" in Canada.

A wealth of current and historical information on these companies is available on their websites. Each company's website is identified after their profile. Readers are encouraged to access these websites to gain a greater understanding of individual companies.

1933 Industries Inc. (OTC: TGIFF) (CSE: TGIF)

1933 Industries Inc. was incorporated in 2008 as Friday Night Inc. and changed its name in September 2018. Its corporate headquarters are in Vancouver, British Columbia. The company engages in the cultivation and production of medical and recreational marijuana in Nevada through American Medicine Association its 100% owned subsidiary. That subsidiary is licensed to cultivate and produce cannabis infused products including edibles. It produces tinctures, lotions, creams, vape pens, cartridges, lip balms, tetrahydrocannabinol concentrates, hemp-seed oils, and capsules under Canna Hemp, Canna Hemp X, Canna Hemp PLUS, Canna Hemp HEMP, and Canna Fused brands. It also sells flower. More information is available at http://1933industries.com

Ackrell SPAC Partners I Company (NASDAQ: ACKIU)

Ackrell is a blank check company (SPAC) formed for the purpose of effecting a merger, capital stock exchange, asset acquisition, stock purchase, reorganization or similar business combination with one or more businesses.

While the Company may pursue an acquisition in any business industry or sector, it intends to concentrate its efforts on identifying businesses in the branded fast-moving consumer goods industry, primarily focusing on the alcoholic and non-alcoholic beverage and wellness sectors, as well as hemp-based branded consumer goods. More information is available at http://ackrell.com

ACREAGE HOLDINGS, INC. (OTC: ACRHF) (CSE: ACRG.A.U)

Acreage Holdings was founded in 2014 and is based in New York, NY. It is a multi-state operator of cannabis cultivation, processing, and distribution facilities in the U.S., including the company's national retail store brand, The Botanist. It markets products under the Botanist, Tweed, Prime, and Innocent brand names. Acreage also owns Universal Hemp, LLC, a hemp subsidiary that markets CBD products throughout the U.S.

On June 27, 2019, Acreage and Canopy Growth signed an agreement whereby Canopy can acquire all the outstanding shares of Acreage stock once federal laws in the United States are changed to either permit the general cultivation, distribution and possession of marijuana or to remove the regulation of such activities from the federal laws of the United States. More information is available at http://acreageholdings.com

Akerna (NASDAQ: KERN)

Akerna Corp. was created by the merger of MTech Acquisition Corp. (a SPAC) and MJ Freeway LLC on June 17, 2019. The company offers MJ Platform, an enterprise resource planning system to the cannabis industry; and Leaf Data Systems, a tracking system designed for government agencies. It also provides consulting services to cannabis industry; business intelligence, an infrastructure as a service tool, which delivers supply chain analytics for the cannabis, hemp, and CBD industries; and Last Call Analytics, a subscription analytics tool for alcohol brands to analyze their retail sales analytics. In addition, the company operates seed-to-sale platform that allows cultivators to track and report various stage of their cannabis growing operations, production, and sales processes. Further, it offers cannabis cultivation management and software to manage and optimize operational workflow in business analytics; and cannabis tracking technology that provides seed-to-sale-to-self data. More information is available at http://akerna.com

Ascend Wellness Holdings (OTC: AAWH) (CSE: AAWH.U)

Ascend Wellness was founded in 2018 and is headquartered in New York, New York. It is a vertically integrated operator with assets and partners in Illinois, Michigan, Ohio,

Massachusetts and New Jersey. Ascend owns and operates cultivation and processing facilities where it grows cannabis strains and produces a curated selection of products. The company's cannabis product categories include flowers, pre-rolls, concentrates, vapes, edibles, and other cannabis-related products. As of March 26, 2021, it operated 13 retail locations. The company also sells its products to third-party licensed cannabis retail stores. More information is available at http://awholdings.com

Aurora Cannabis Inc. (NASDAQ: ACB) (TSX: ACB)

Aurora Cannabis is the third largest Canadian licensed producer "LP" as measured by market capitalization. It is headquartered in Edmonton, Canada and was among the first companies to be licensed in Canada. It cultivates, processes, and distributes cannabis products worldwide.

It is vertically integrated and horizontally diversified across various segments of the cannabis value chain, including facility engineering and design, cannabis breeding, genetics research, production, derivatives, home cultivation, wholesale, and retail distribution. The company produces various strains of dried cannabis, cannabis oil and capsules, and topical kits for medical patients. It also sells vaporizers; consumable vaporizer accessories, including valves, screens, etc.; and herb mills for using CanniMed herbal cannabis products, as well as grinders and vaporizer lockable containers. In addition, the company engages in the development of medical cannabis products at various stages of development, including oral, topical, edible, and inhalable products; and operation of CanvasRX, a network of cannabis counseling and outreach centers. Further, it provides patient counseling services; design and construction services; and cannabis analytical product testing services. The company's brand portfolio includes Aurora, Aurora Drift, San Rafael '71, Daily Special, AltaVie, MedReleaf, CanniMed, Whistler, Woodstock, and ROAR Sports. More information is available at http://auroramj.com

Ayr Wellness (OTC: AYRWF) (CSE: AYR.A)

Ayr Wellness began its corporate life as Cannabis Strategies Acquisition Corporation, a special purpose acquisition corporation "SPAC" formed in late 2017. In May 2019 it changed its name to Ayr Strategies, Inc. when it completed its qualifying transaction and became a vertically-integrated cannabis multi-state operator. It cultivates, extracts, manufactures, distributes, and retails cannabis products and branded cannabis packaged goods. The company's cannabis and cannabis products include concentrates, edibles, and vaporizer products. It also provides administrative, consulting, and operations support services to licensed cannabis companies. In addition, Ayr Wellness Inc. operates medical retail dispensaries. More information is available at http://ayrwellness.com

Bespoke Capital Acquisition Corp (NASDAQ: VWE)

BCAC is special purpose acquisition corporation (SPAC) formed for the purpose of effecting an acquisition of one or more businesses within a specified period of time. It intends to focus its search for target businesses in the cannabis industry; however, it is not limited to a particular industry or geographic region for purposes of completing its qualifying transaction. Bespoke intends to identify and execute on a qualifying acquisition by leveraging its network to find attractive investment opportunities as it seeks to acquire several complementary companies as part of its qualifying acquisition to form a leading vertically integrated international cannabis company, with a "land to brand" strategy and global reach. On June 7, 2021 it merged with Vintage Wine Estates and began trading on the NASDAQ under the symbol VWE. More information is available at http://bespokecp.com

BGP Acquisition Corp. (OTC: BGPPF)

On February 4, 2021, BGP Acquisition Corp. completed its initial public offering of 11,500,000 class A restricted voting units ("Class A Restricted Voting Units") (including 1,500,000 Class A Restricted Voting Units issued pursuant to the exercise in full of the over-allotment option) at an offering price of US$10.00 per Class a Restricted Voting Unit, for gross proceeds of US$115,000,000. BGP is a special purpose acquisition corporation incorporated under the laws of the Province of British Columbia for the purpose of effecting, directly or indirectly, an acquisition of one or more businesses or assets, by way of a merger, amalgamation, arrangement, share exchange, asset acquisition, share purchase, reorganization, or any other similar business combination within a specified period of time (a "Qualifying Transaction"). It intends to focus its search for target businesses that are involved in cannabis and/or related sectors; however, it is not limited to a particular industry or geographic region for purposes of completing its Qualifying Transaction. More information is available in the following SEDAR filing: https://www.SEDAR.com/GetFile.do?lang=EN&docClass=9&issuerNo=00051263&issuerType=03&projectNo=03160438&docId=4877878

Body and Mind Inc. (OTC: BMMJ)

Body and Mind Inc. was formerly known as Deploy Technologies Inc. and changed its name to Body and Mind Inc. in November 2017. The company is headquartered in Vancouver, British Columbia. It cultivates, produces, processes, distributes, and retails medical and recreational cannabis in Nevada, California, Arkansas, and Ohio. The company offers packaged and grinded flower buds; concentrates; disposable pen vaporizers; distillate oil cartridges; and distillate infused edible products. It produces and sells cannabis flowers, oil extracts, and edibles under the Body and Mind brand name. The company also operates ShowGrow San Diego dispensary; and manages ShowGrow Long Beach dispensary. In addition, it is involved in the production of marijuana extract products, such as distillate oils, ice waxes, dry sifts, shatters, edibles, and topicals.

More information is available at http://bamcannabis.com

C21 Investments Inc. (OTC: CXXIF) (CSE: CXXI)

C21 Investments is based in Vancouver, Canada. It is a vertically integrated cannabis company that cultivates, processes, and distributes quality cannabis and hemp-derived consumer products in the United States. The Company is focused on the acquisition and integration of core retail, manufacturing, and distribution assets in strategic markets that offer high-growth potential. The Company owns Silver State Relief and Silver State Cultivation in Nevada, and Phantom Farms, Eco Firma Farms in Oregon. These brands produce and distribute a broad range of THC and CBD products from cannabis flowers, pre-rolls, cannabis oil, vaporizer cartridges and edibles. More information is available at http://cxxi.ca

Canaccord Genuity Growth Corp

Canaccord Genuity Growth Corp. is a newly organized special purpose acquisition corporation (SPAC) incorporated under the laws of the Province of Ontario for the purpose of effecting a qualifying transaction within a specified period of time. The sponsor of CGGC is CG Investments Inc. ("CGII"), a wholly-owned subsidiary of Canaccord Genuity Group Inc. and an affiliate of Canaccord Genuity Corp. ("Canaccord Genuity"). CGII's position in CGGC was acquired for investment purposes.

CGII is restricted from selling its Class B Shares and Class B Units as described in the Final Prospectus. CGII may purchase and/or sell any Class a Restricted Voting Units it acquires from time to time, subject to applicable law. More information is available at http://canaccordgenuity.com

Canopy Growth Corporation (NASDAQ: CGC) (TSX: WEED)

Canopy Growth is the largest cannabis company in the world as measured by market capitalization. It started in 2014 as Tweed Marijuana Inc. and was among the first companies awarded a Canadian LP license. In 2015 it changed its name to Canopy Growth Corporation.

It is headquartered in Smiths Falls, Canada. It engages in the production, distribution, and sale of cannabis and hemp-based products for recreational and medical purposes primarily in Canada, the United States, and Germany. It operates through two segments, Global Cannabis and Other Consumer Products. The company's products include dried cannabis flowers, oils and concentrates, and softgel capsules. It offers its products under the Tweed, Quatreau, Deep Space, Spectrum Therapeutics, First & Free, TWD, This Works, BioSteel, DNA Genetics CraftGrow, Tokyo Smoke, DOJA, Van der Pop, and Bean & Bud brands. The company also provides growth capital and a strategic support platform that pursues investment opportunities in the global cannabis sector.

Canopy Growth Corporation has a clinical research partnership with NEEKA Health Canada and NHL Alumni Association to examine the efficacy of CBD-based therapies as part of the mitigation of persistent post-concussion symptoms. Canopy Growth has entered into the health and wellness consumer space in key markets including Canada, the United States, and Europe through BioSteel sports nutrition, and This Works skin and sleep solutions; and has introduced additional federally-permissible CBD products to the United States through its First & Free and Martha Stewart CBD brands. Canopy Growth has an established partnership with Fortune 500 alcohol leader Constellation Brands. For more information is available at http://canopygrowth.com

Cansortium Inc. (OTC: CNTMF) (CSE: TIUM.U)

Cansortium was incorporated in 2018 and is headquartered in Miami, Florida. It is a vertically-integrated cannabis company with licenses and operations in Florida, Pennsylvania, Michigan and Texas. The company operates under the Fluent™ brand and its cannabis products are offered in oral drops, capsules, suppositories, topicals, syringes, dried flower, prerolls, cartridges, and edibles. More information is available at http://getfluent.com

Captor Capital Corp. (CSE: CPTR)

Captor Capital Corp. is based in Toronto, Canada and was formed in June 2017. It engages in the manufacture and retail sale of cannabis products in the United States. It operates two dispensaries under the CHAI Cannabis Co. brand in Santa Cruz and Monterey, California, as well as operates an e-commerce site under the CHAI-brand. More information is available at http://captorcapital.com

Ceres Acquisition Corporation (OTC: CERAF)

Ceres is a special purpose acquisition corporation "SPAC" incorporated in 2020 under the laws of the Province of British Columbia for the purpose of effecting an acquisition of one or more businesses or assets, by way of a merger, amalgamation, arrangement, share exchange, asset acquisition, share purchase, reorganization, or any other similar business combination. It is headquartered in Los Angeles, California.

On February 21, 2021, Ceres and SH Parent, Inc., one of the largest privately-held multi-state cannabis operators in the United States doing business as Parallel, entered into a definitive business combination agreement or qualifying transaction. In addition, a group of investors participated by acquiring an equity offering of non-voting common stock at U.S.$10.00 per share for aggregate gross proceeds of U.S.$228.5 million. More information is available at http://ceresacquisition.com

Chalice Brands Ltd. (OTC: CHALF) (CSE: CHAL)

Chalice Brands is headquartered in Portland, Oregon. It was previously known as Golden Leaf Holdings Ltd and traded under the symbol GLDFF until June 3, 2021. Chalice produces, processes, and distributes cannabis via wholesale and retail channels including seven dispensaries in Portland, Oregon. The company operates nationally through Fifth and Root. It has operations in Oregon and California. More information is available at http:// investors.chalicebrandsltd.com

Choice Consolidation Corp. (OTC: CDXXF)

Choice Consolidation Corp. is a special purpose acquisition company ("SPAC") targeting an acquisition of one or more cannabis businesses or assets that can create a best-in-class cannabis multi-state operator ("MSO"). Choice is headquartered in Chicago, Illinois. It intends to search for businesses with a focus on cannabis cultivation, production, distribution, brands, manufacturing and/or retailing businesses in key limited license markets in the US. The CEO of Choice co-founded Cresco Labs, one of the largest vertically integrated MSOs in the United States and served as its President until March 2020. More information is available at http://choiceconsol.com

Clover Leaf Capital Corp

Clover Leaf Capital Corp. is a blank check company (SPAC) formed for the purpose of effecting a merger, capital stock exchange, asset acquisition, stock purchase, reorganization or similar business combination with one or more businesses in an initial business combination. While it may pursue a business combination target in any business, industry or geographic region, it intends to focus its search on businesses in the legalized cannabis industry. At the time of its formation it had not selected any specific business combination target and it had not had any substantive discussions, directly or indirectly, with any business combination target. On April 7, 2021 it filed an S-1 registration statement with the SEC announcing its intention to sell up to 14,375,000 units at a price of $10 per unit in an IPO with redeemable warrants attached.

The SPAC sponsor is controlled by Yntegra Capital Management LLC of Miami, Florida, which is part of the Yntegra Group, a family office and multi-service provider that specializes in high yield transactions that has managed over $1 billion in commodities trading activity and placement of over $100 million in private equity investments. More information is available in the following URL, which contains the S-1 filing submitted to the SEC.
https://www.sec.gov/Archives/edgar/data/1849058/000121390021020691/fs12021_cloverleafcap.htm

Columbia Care Inc. (OTC: CCHWF) (CSE: CCHW)

Columbia Care was founded in 2012 and is one of the original providers of medical cannabis in the United States. It is headquartered in New York, NY and was acquired by in a SPAC qualifying transaction by Canaccord Genuity Growth Corporation. It cultivates, produces and distributes medical and adult use cannabis products. It is licensed in 19 U.S. jurisdictions and the European Union. Columbia Care operates 122 facilities including 92 dispensaries and 30 cultivation and manufacturing facilities. Columbia Care has expanded into the adult use market. The company currently offers products spanning flower, edibles, oils, capsules and tablets, and manufactures brands including Seed & Strain, Amber and Platinum Label CBD. Columbia Care has engaged in more than four million transactions since it began sales. More information is available at http://col-care.com

Cresco Labs Inc. (OTC: CRLBF) (CSE: CL)

Cresco Labs is headquartered in Chicago, Illinois and its market capitalization is among the ten largest vertically integrated, multistate cannabis companies in the United States. It cultivates, manufactures, and sells cannabis products in the form of flowers, vape pens, live resins, disposable pens, and extracts under the Cresco brand; flowers, popcorns, shakes, pre-rolls, and vapes under the High Supply brand; flowers, vapes, and edibles under the Good News brand; vapes and edibles under the Wonder Wellness Co brand; and tinctures, capsules, salves, ingestibles, sublingual oils, and transdermal patches under the Remedi brand, as well as cannabis products made from plants under the Reserve brand. The company also offers cannabis flowers under the FloraCal brand; and chocolate and toffee confections, fruit-forward gummies, hard sweets, and taffy under the Mindy's Edibles brand, as well as licenses the Kiva brand, which produces cannabis infused edibles, including chocolate confections, gummies, mints, and tarts. Cresco Labs operates a Social Equity and Educational Development initiative "SEED" to ensure that all members of society have the skills, knowledge and opportunity to work and own businesses in the cannabis industry. More information is available at http://crescolabs.com

Cronos Group (NASDAQ: CRON)

Cronos Group was founded in 2012 and is one of Canada's original licensed producers. It is a global cannabinoid company with international production and distribution across five continents with headquarters in Toronto, Canada. It manufactures, markets, and distributes hemp-derived supplements and cosmetic products through e-commerce, retail, and hospitality partner channels under the Lord Jones and Happy Dance brands in the United States. The company is also involved in the cultivation, manufacture, and marketing of cannabis and cannabis-derived products for the medical and adult-use markets. It sells cannabis and cannabis products, including dried cannabis, pre-rolls, and cannabis extracts through wholesale and direct-to-client channels under its wellness platform, PEACE NATURALS; and operates under two adult-use brands, COVE and Spinach. The company also exports dried cannabis and cannabis oils to Germany, Israel, and Australia.

In December 2018 Altria (MO) bought a 45% ownership position in Cronos for $1.8 billion. Altria also acquired a warrant allowing it to increase its position to about 55% at a price of $19 per share. Altria manufactures and sells cigarettes, oral tobacco products, and wine in the United States. Its brands include Marlboro, Black & Mild, Copenhagen, Skoal, Red Seal, and Husky. The company also produces and sells under the Chateau Ste. Michelle and 14 Hands wines.

It imports and markets Antinori, Torres, and Villa Maria Estate wines, as well as Nicolas Feuillatte Champagne in the United States. More information is available at http://thecronosgroup.com

Curaleaf Holdings Inc. (OTC: CURLF) (CSE: CURA)

Curaleaf was founded in 2010 and is headquartered in Wakefield, Massachusetts. It has operations in 23 states with 106 dispensaries, 23 cultivation sites and over 30 processing sites. It operates in two segments, Cannabis Operations and Non-Cannabis Operations. The Cannabis Operations segment engages in the production and sale of cannabis through retail and wholesale channels. The Non-Cannabis Operations segment provides professional services, including cultivation, processing, and retail know-how and back-office administration, intellectual property licensing, real estate leasing services, and lending facilities to medical and adult-use cannabis licensees under management service agreements. It offers oil-based formulations, such as vaporizing, cartridges, tinctures, and capsules; and ground-flower. The company also provides hemp-based CBD products. More information is available at http://curaleaf.com

4Front Ventures Corp. (OTCQX: FFNTF) (CSE: FFNT)

4Front was founded in 2011 and is headquartered in Phoenix, Arizona. It cultivates, manufactures, and distributes THC Cannabis and CBD products in California, Illinois, Massachusetts, Michigan, and Washington. Its product portfolio includes over 21 cannabis brands including Marmas, Crystal Clear, Funky Monkey, Pebbles, and the Pure Ratios wellness collection. Products are distributed through retail outlets and 4Front's chain of Mission branded dispensaries. In addition, the company sells equipment, supplies, and intellectual property to cannabis producers; imports and sale equipment and supplies; leases real estate properties to cannabis producers; offers consulting services; and operates cannabis dispensaries. More information is available at http://4frontventures.com

Gage Growth Corp. (OTC: GAEGF) (CSE: GAGE)

The company was originally incorporated in 2017 as Wolverine Partners Corp. but changed its name to Gage Growth Corp. in October 2020. It is headquartered in Toronto, Canada. It is a single-state-operator "SSO" with cultivation, manufacturing, and distribution in Michigan. It operates three cultivation facilities and eight dispensaries. Gage's portfolio includes city and state approvals for 19 cultivation licenses, three processing licenses and 13 dispensaries. More information is available at http://gagecannabis.com

Goodness Growth Holdings (OTC: GDNSF) (CSE: GDNS)

Goodness Growth was formerly known as Vireo Health International, Inc. (OTC: VREOF) and changed its name in June 2021. It is a physician-led cannabis company headquartered in Minneapolis, Minnesota. It cultivates cannabis; manufactures pharmaceutical-grade cannabis extracts; and sells its products through its network of Green Goods and other retail locations, and third-party dispensaries. The company grows and/or processes cannabis in eight markets and operates 16 dispensaries. More information is available at http://vireohealth.com

Glass House Group (OTC: MRCQF)

The Glass House Group is headquartered in California and is a fully integrated cannabis company that cultivates, processes, and distributes marijuana and hemp. In April 2021 it agreed to be acquired by a SPAC, Mercer Brand Acquisition Corporation, in a qualifying transaction for $567 million. Glass House is in the process of converting a 5.5 million square foot greenhouse complex on 140 acres in Ventura, CA into a cannabis cultivation facility. Once the conversion is complete, the company will have 6 million square feet of cultivation. The greenhouse complex now grows tomatoes and cucumbers. More information is available at http://glasshousegroup.com

Greenlane Holdings Inc. (OTC: GNLN)

Greenlane was founded in 2005 and is headquartered in Boca Raton, Florida. It sells cannabis accessories, child-resistant packaging, and specialty vaporization products in the United States, Canada, Europe, Australia, and South America. The company provides vaporizers, liquid nicotine, storage solutions, pipes, apparel lines, and consumption accessories, as well as bubblers, rigs, and other smoking and vaporization related accessories and merchandise. It offers its products under the VIBES rolling papers, Pollen Gear, the Marley Natural accessory line, Aerospaced & Groove grinders, K. Haring Glass Collections, Eyce specialty silicone smoking products, and Higher Standards brands. The company also operates e-commerce websites, such as Vapor.com, Higherstandards.com, Aerospaced.com, Canada.vapor.com, Vaposhop.com, and others. It serves smoke shops, dispensaries, and specialty retail stores. More information is available at http://gnln.com

Greenrose Acquisition Corp. (OTC: GNRS)

Greenrose Acquisition Corp. is based in Amityville, NY. It is a blank check company organized for the purpose of effecting a merger, share exchange, asset acquisition, stock purchase, recapitalization, reorganization, or other similar business combination with one or more businesses or entities in the cannabis industry. It originally listed on the Nasdaq as a SPAC; however, it delisted its shares on the Nasdaq on June 21, 2021 and transferred its listing to the OTCQX Best Market. The transfer was necessitated by the fact that upon closing its qualifying transaction Greenrose would become a U.S. cannabis company with plant-touching operations and would no longer be in compliance with Nasdaq Rules. More information is available at http://greenrosecorp.com

Green Thumb Industries (OTC: GTBIF) (CSE: GTII)

Green Thumb was established in2014 and is headquartered in Chicago, Illinois. It is among the largest MSOs with a multi-billion dollars market capitalization. It cultivates, manufactures, and distributes cannabis products across the United States. Green Thumb's portfolio of branded cannabis products includes Beboe, Dogwalkers, Dr. Solomon's, incredibles, Rythm and The Feel Collection. The company owns and operates retail cannabis stores called Rise™. It has 13 manufacturing facilities, licenses for 97 retail locations and operations across 12 U.S. markets. More information is available at http://GTIgrows.com

GrowGeneration Corporation (NASDAQ: GRWG)

GrowGeneration was founded in 2008 as Easylife Corp and is headquartered in Denver, Colorado. It owns and operates specialty retail hydroponic and organic gardening centers. GrowGen has 55 stores, which include 20 locations in California, 8 locations in Colorado, 7 locations in Michigan, 5 locations in Maine, 5 locations in Oklahoma, 2 locations in Nevada, 2 locations in Washington, 2 locations in Oregon, 1 location in Arizona, 1 location in Rhode Island,1 location in Florida, and 1 location in Massachusetts.
GrowGen also operates an online superstore for cultivators at http://growgeneration.com and B2B ERP platform, http://agron.io. GrowGen carries and sells thousands of products, including organic nutrients and soils, advanced lighting technology and state of the art hydroponic equipment to be used indoors and outdoors by commercial and home growers. More information is available at https://ir.growgeneration.com

Grown Rogue International (OTC: GRUSF) (CSE: GRIN)

Grown Rogue International Inc. is based in Toronto, Canada. It is engaged in the cultivation, production, and wholesale of cannabis products in Oregon and Michigan. The company offers flower products, such as indicas, sativas, and hybrids; and edibles, vape cartridges, pre-rolls, and concentrates. It sells its products directly to dispensaries. More information is available at https://www.grownrogue.com/

Greenrose Acquisition Corp. (OTC: GNRS)

Greenrose is a blank check company, also known as a Special Purpose Acquisition Corporation ("SPAC") formed under the laws of the State of Delaware on August 26, 2019. It was formed for the purpose of entering into a merger, share exchange, asset acquisition, stock purchase, recapitalization, reorganization or other similar business combination with one or more businesses or entities. Its search focused on the cannabis industry. Greenhouse issued an aggregate of 4,312,500 shares of common stock ("Founder's Shares") for an aggregate purchase price of $25,000, or approximately $0.006 per share, to our sponsor, Greenrose Associates LLC, a New York limited liability company ("Sponsor").

On February 13, 2020, Greenhouse consummated an initial public offering ("IPO") of 15,000,000 of our units ("Public Units"). Each Public Unit consists of one share of common stock and one redeemable warrant, with each warrant entitling the holder to purchase one share of common stock at a price of $11.50 per share. The Public Units were sold at an offering price of $10.00 per Public Unit, generating gross proceeds of $150,000,000.

Simultaneously with the consummation of the IPO, Greenhouse consummated a private placement ("Private Placement") of 300,000 units ("Private Units") at a price of $10.00 per Private Unit and 1,500,000 warrants ("Private Warrants") at a price of $1.00 per Private Warrant, generating total proceeds of $4,500,000. The Private Units and Private Warrants were sold to the Sponsor and Imperial Capital, LLC. The Private Units and Private Warrants are identical to the Public Units and warrants sold in the IPO, except that the Private Warrants and the warrants underlying the Private Units are non-redeemable and may be exercised on a cashless basis, in each case so long as they continue to be held by the initial purchasers or their permitted transferee.

On February 14, 2020, Greenhouse consummated the sale of an additional 2,250,000 Public Units that were subject to the underwriters' over-allotment option at $10.00 per Public Unit, generating gross proceeds of $22,500,000. Simultaneously with the closing of the sale of the additional Public Units, Greenhouse consummated the sale of an additional 30,000 Private Units at $10.00 per Private Unit and 150,000 Private Warrants, at a price of $1.00 per Private Warrant, generating total proceeds of $450,000. Following the closing of the over-allotment option and sale of additional Private Units and Private Warrants, an aggregate amount of $172,500,000 has been placed in the trust account established in connection with the IPO. As a result of the underwriters' exercise of the over-allotment option in full, 562,500 of the Founder's Shares are no longer subject to forfeiture. More information is available at https://investharborside.com

Harborside Inc. (OTC: HBORF) (CSE: HBOR)

Harborside was founded in 2006 and is headquartered in Oakland, California. It was among the first companies to be awarded a medical cannabis license in the United States. It cultivates, manufactures, distributes, and sells cannabis and cannabis products.

Harborside owns and operates three retail dispensaries in the San Francisco Bay Area, a dispensary in the Palm Springs area, a dispensary in Oregon and a cultivation/production facility in Salinas, California. The company sells its products under the Harborside, Harborside Farms, Harborside Farms Reserve, and KEY brands. More information is available at https://investharborside.com

Harvest Health & Recreation Inc. (OTC: HRVSF) (CSE: HARV)

Harvest Health was founded in 2011 and is headquartered in Tempe, Arizona. It is a vertically integrated cannabis company and multi-state operator. It cultivates, processes, and sells inhalable, ingestible, and topical cannabis products in the United States. The company offers cannabis oil products; inhalables, including flower, dabbable concentrates, pre-filled vaporizer pens, and cartridges; and capsules, tinctures, and cannabis product edibles, including chocolates, gummies, mints, fruit chews, and dissolvable mouth strips under the Avenue, CBX SCIENCES, EVOLAB, ALCHEMY, CHROMA, CO2LORS, GOODSUN, MODERN FLOWER, and ROLL ONE brand names. It also operates retail dispensaries that sell proprietary and third-party cannabis products to patients and customers. More information is available at http://harvesthoc.com

Hollister Biosciences Inc. (OTC: HSTRF) (CSE: HOLL)

Hollister Biosciences Inc. was incorporated in 2019 and is based in Vancouver, British Columbia, Canada. Together with its subsidiaries, manufactures and distributes recreational cannabis and cannabis products in California and Arizona. It offers pre rolls, infused pre rolls, vape formulation, vape cart filling, tinctures, and capsules, as well as hash and crumble infused under HashBone, Purity Petibles, Mighty Med Vape, NanoPure, and Rebel Hemp Company brands, as well as contract manufacturing white label products for other companies. The company has a collaboration with Tommy Chong's Cannabis, Tactical Relief, and CLOWN. More information is available at http://hollistercannabisco.com

Hydrofarm Holdings Group, Inc. (NASDAQ: HYFM)

Hydrofarm Holdings was founded in 1977 and is based in Fairless Hills, Pennsylvania. It engages in the manufacture and distribution of controlled environment agriculture (CEA) equipment and supplies in the United States and Canada. The company offers agricultural lighting devices, indoor climate control equipment, hydroponics and nutrients, and plant additives used to grow, farm, and cultivate cannabis, flowers, fruits, plants, vegetables, grains, and herbs in controlled environment; and distributes CEA equipment and supplies, which include grow light systems; heating, ventilation, and air conditioning systems; humidity and carbon dioxide monitors and controllers; water pumps, heaters, chillers, and filters; nutrient and fertilizer delivery systems; and various growing media made from soil, rock wool or coconut fiber.

It also provides hydroponics systems, such as hydro systems, hydro trays and components, meters and solutions, pumps and irrigation systems, water filtration systems, pots and containers, and tents and tarps; atmospheric control equipment comprising controllers, monitors and timers, ventilation/air conditioning equipment, air purification equipment, and CO2 equipment; and nutrients and additives. The company offers its products under the PHOTOBIO, Phantom, Quantum, Digilux, Jump Start, Active Aqua, Active Air, Autopilot, Xtrasun, Active Eye, Agrobrite, GROW!T, Phat, and oxyClone brands. More information is available at http://hydrofarm.com

iAnthus Capital Holdings, Inc. (OTC: ITHUF) (CSE: IAN)

iAnthus is headquartered in New York, NY. It owns and operates licensed cannabis cultivation, processing, and dispensary facilities in the United States. It offers biomass products, such as pre-rolls; cannabis infused products, including topical creams and edibles; vape cartridges, concentrates, live resins, wax products, oils, and tinctures; cannabidiol products, such as topical creams, tinctures, and sprays, as well as products for beauty and skincare that include lotions, creams, haircare products, lip balms, and bath bombs. The company engages in the wholesale-distribution and retail of CBD products.

It owns and/or operates 31 dispensaries and 10 cultivation and/or processing facilities in 9 states. More information is available at http://ianthus.com

Innovative Industrial Properties (NYSE: IIPR)

Innovative Industrial Properties, Inc. is a self-advised Maryland corporation focused on the acquisition, ownership and management of specialized properties leased to experienced, state-licensed operators for their regulated medical-use cannabis facilities. Innovative Industrial Properties, Inc. has elected to be taxed as a real estate investment trust, commencing with the year ended December 31, 2017. More information is available at http://innovativeindustrialproperties.com

Item 9 Labs Corp. (OTC: INLB)

Item 9 Labs Corp. is headquartered in Phoenix, Arizona. It operates as a vertically integrated cannabis operator and dispensary franchisor in the United States. The company produces cannabis and cannabis-related products in various categories, such as flower; concentrates; distillates; and hardware. It offers products through licensed dispensaries to consumers in Arizona. More information is available at https://www.item9labscorp.com

Jazz Pharmaceuticals plc (NASDAQ: JAZZ)

Jazz Pharmaceuticals plc was founded in 2003 and is headquartered in Dublin, Ireland. It is a global biopharmaceutical company dedicated to identifying, developing and commercializing pharmaceutical products for various unmet medical needs worldwide.

The company has a portfolio of products and product candidates with a focus in the areas of neuroscience, including sleep medicine and movement disorders; and in oncology, including hematologic and solid tumors. On May 5, 2021 it completed the acquisition of GW Pharmaceuticals, the only company that had at that time received FDA and DEA approval to market a plant-based cannabis drug in the United States. More information is available at http://jazzpharmaceuticals.com

Jushi Holdings Inc. (OTC: JUSHF) (CSE: JUSH)

Jushi was founded in 2018 and is headquartered in Boca Raton, Florida. It is a cannabis and hemp company engaged in the cultivation, processing, retail, and distribution of medical and adult-use products. It focuses on building a portfolio of branded cannabis and hemp-derived assets in various jurisdictions in California, Illinois, Ohio, Pennsylvania, Nevada, and Virginia.

The company operates 11 retail locations under the BEYOND/HELLO retail brand, which include 8 medical dispensaries in Ardmore, Bristol, Johnstown, Philadelphia, Reading, Scranton, and West Chester, Pennsylvania; and 2 adult-use and medical dispensaries located in Sauget and Normal, Illinois. It also offers hemp-based CBD products under the Nira brand. More information is available at http://jushi.com

KushCo Holdings (OTC: KSHB)

KushCo Holdings, Inc. was founded in 2010 as Kush Bottles, Inc. and changed its name in 2018. Its headquarters are in Cypress, California. KushCo markets and sells packaging products, vaporizers, solvents, accessories, and branding solutions to customers operating in the regulated medical and adult recreational cannabis and hemp-derived cannabidiol (CBD) industries in the United States, Canada, and internationally. Its principal products include bottles, jars, bags, tubes, containers, vape cartridges, vape batteries and accessories, labels and processing supplies, solvents, natural products, stainless steel tanks, and custom branded anti-counterfeit and authentication labels. The company also offers hemp trading and retail services. The company sells products to the business-to-business market, which includes brand owners, farmers, growers, processors, producers, distributors, and licensed retailers in states with legal medical and/or adult recreational use cannabis programs and legal CBD programs through its direct sales force and e-commerce website. More information is available at http://kushco.com

Lowell Farms Inc. (CSE: LOWL; OTCQX: LOWLF)

Indus Holdings Inc. was founded in 2014 and in early 2021 it acquired the Lowell Herb Co. and Lowell Smokes trademark brands, product portfolio, and production assets from The Hacienda Group. In that process Indus changed its corporate name to Lowell Farms Inc. and the OTC stock symbol was changed from INDXF to LOWLF. The company is a Salinas, California based vertically-integrated cannabis company that incorporates cultivation, extraction, manufacturing, brand sales, marketing, and distribution.

Lowell Farms produces an extensive portfolio of original and licensed brands, including Lowell Herb Co., Cypress Cannabis, MOON, and Kaizen Extracts, for licensed retailers statewide. More information is available at http://lowellfarms.com

MariMed (OTC: MRMD)

MariMed Advisors was founded in 2012 to advise operators and licensees on the design, development, operations, and financing of new cannabis cultivation centers and dispensaries nationwide.

That business evolved into MariMed Inc, a seed-to-consumer vertically integrated multi state operator. The company used its experience as an advisor to develop and acquire its own brands of cannabis precision dosed products and cannabis facilities. It now has 17 cannabis licenses in six states and manages more than 300,000 square feet of cannabis facilities. More information is available at http://marimedinc.com

Medicine Man (OTC: SHWZ)

Medicine Man was founded in 2009 as an avenue to produce medical marijuana in the area of Denver, Colorado. In 2014, Medicine Man opened its doors to recreational customers. It now has dispensaries in Denver, Aurora, Thornton, and Longmont, Colorado. It offers a full array of high potency concentrates, pre-rolls, infused edibles, topicals, transdermals, tinctures, and more THC and CBD products. More information is available at http://medicinemandenver.com

MedMen Enterprises Inc. (OTC: MMNFF) (CSE: MMEN)

MedMen Enterprises was founded in 2010 and is headquartered in Culver City, California. It cultivates, produces, distributes, and retails recreational and medicinal cannabis under the LuxLyte and MedMen Red brand names. It operates 25 retail stores in Arizona, California, Florida, Illinois, Massachusetts, and Nevada. It offers assorted cannabis products including its own brands through its retail stores, via delivery service, as well as curbside and in-store pick up. More information is available at http://medmen.com

Mercer Park Brand Acquisition Corp. (OTC: MRCQF)

Mercer Park was incorporated in 2019 and is headquartered in New York, NY. It is a SPAC, special purpose acquisition company, that was established to effect an acquisition of one or more businesses or assets by way of a merger, amalgamation, arrangement, share exchange, asset acquisition, share purchase, reorganization, or any other similar business combination involving the Corporation in cannabis and/or cannabis-adjacent industries. Mercer Park, the SPAC sponsor, is a limited partnership indirectly controlled by Mercer Park, L.P., a privately-held family office based in New York, New York.

Mercer Park is closely associated with Ayr Wellness and has the same office address at 590 Madison Avenue, 26th Floor, in New York City. On April 8, 2021 it announced a definitive agreement (which was later amended) to merge with Glass House Group, Inc., a California company in the cannabis business. More information is available at http://mercerparkbrand.com

Merida Merger Corp. I (NASDAQ: MCMJ)

Merida Merger Corp. I is a blank check company formed for the purpose of entering into a merger, share exchange, asset acquisition, stock purchase, recapitalization, reorganization or other similar business combination with one or more businesses or entities. Its headquarters are in New York City and it targets businesses in the cannabis industry. More information is available at http://meridacap.com

MTech Acquisition Corp. (NASDAQ: KERN)

MTech Acquisition Corp. claim it is the first U.S. listed Special Purpose Acquisition Company (SPAC) focused on acquiring businesses ancillary to the cannabis industry. In June 2019 it combined with MJ Freeway LLC, a seed-to-sale regulatory compliance technology provider and developer of an enterprise resource planning (ERP) platform for the cannabis industry. The combination was named Akerna Company.

Akerna Corp. operates as a technology company. The company offers MJ Platform, an enterprise resource planning system to the cannabis industry; and Leaf Data Systems, a tracking system designed for government agencies. It also provides consulting services to cannabis industry; business intelligence, an infrastructure as a service tool, which delivers supply chain analytics for the cannabis, hemp, and CBD industries; and Last Call Analytics, a subscription analytics tool for alcohol brands to analyze their retail sales analytics. In addition, the company operates seed-to-sale platform that allows cultivators to track and report various stage of their cannabis growing operations, production, and sales processes. Further, it offers cannabis cultivation management and software to manage and optimize operational workflow in business analytics; and cannabis tracking technology that provides seed-to-sale-to-self data. More information is available at http://akerna.com

Next Green Wave Holdings Inc. (OTC: NXGWF) (CSE: NGW)

Next Green Wave, which was incorporated in 2011, was known as Crossgate Capital Corporation before changing its name in August 2018. It is headquartered in Vancouver, British Columbia. It cultivates and distributes medicinal and recreational cannabis in California. It is also involved in the processing, production, and packaging of dry flower, cannabis oils, and concentrates. The company offers its products under the Loki the Dog, Carey Hart, King Louie, Sketchy Tank, Junkyard, SD Cannabis, Thorn St. Brewing, Toy Machine Co, and Junkyard brands.

The Company owns and operates a 35,000 sq. ft. indoor facility in Coalinga, CA, which is home to its nursery, cultivation, distribution, and extraction business. More information is available at http://nextgreenwave.com

Northern Lights Acquisition Corp. (NASDAQ: NLITU)

Northern Lights is a Denver, Colorado headquartered special acquisition company (SPAC) formed in Delaware in February 2021. It is focused on the cannabis industry. One of its two CEOs co-founded One Cannabis Group, a retail cannabis franchiser, which was acquired by Item 9 Labs. More information is available at http://sec.gov

Parallel (OTC: CERAF) (NEO: CERE.U)

Surterra Wellness was founded in 2014 and is headquartered in Atlanta, GA. In 2021 it became Parallel via a qualifying SPAC transaction with Ceres Acquisition Corporation.

Parallel is a vertically integrated, multi-state cannabis companies in the United States. It has operations in four medical and adult-use markets under the retail brands of Surterra Wellness in Florida; goodblend in Texas; New England Treatment Access (NETA) in Massachusetts, and The Apothecary Shoppe in Nevada. Parallel also has a license under its goodblend Pennsylvania brand for vertically integrated operations and up to six retail locations in Pennsylvania, in addition to a medical cannabis research partnership with the University of Pittsburgh School of Medicine. Parallel added Illinois as a sixth market when its acquired six Windy City Cannabis licenses. Parallel's product portfolio of proprietary and licensed consumer brands includes Surterra Wellness, Coral Reefer, Float and Heights. Parallel operates approximately 50 locations nationwide, including 42 retail stores, and cultivation and manufacturing sites.

Through its wholly-owned Parallel Biosciences subsidiary, it conducts advanced cannabis science and R&D for new product development in its facilities in Massachusetts, Florida, Texas and a facility in Budapest, Hungary through an exclusive license and partnership. More information is available at http://liveparallel.com

Planet 13 (OTC: PLNHF) (CSE: PLTH)

Planet 13 was incorporated in 2002 and is headquartered in Las Vegas, Nevada. It is a vertically integrated cannabis company that cultivates, produces, distributes, and markets cannabis and cannabis-infused and related products for medical and retail cannabis markets. It also operates dispensaries that provide cannabis, cannabis extracts, and infused products. In addition, the company provides cardholder process navigation services; individual consultations; compassionate care programs; patient education services; express services; and home delivery services. Further, it operates a coffee shop and pizzeria. The company offers its products under the Planet 13, Medizin, TRENDI, Leaf & Vine, HaHa, and Dreamland Chocolates brands. More information is available at http://planet13holdings.com

Plus Products Inc. (OTC: PLPRF) (CSE: PLUS)

Plus Products Inc. was incorporated in 2018 and is based in San Mateo, California. It develops, manufactures, and sells cannabis products in California. The company offers cannabis-infused edibles to the regulated medicinal and adult-use, or recreational markets. It sells products under the PLUS brand to dispensaries and delivery service customers. It launched a national hemp CBD product line that is available in 43 states in the U.S. More information is available at http://plusproducts.com

Red White & Bloom Brands Inc. (OTC: RWBYF) (CSE: RWB)

The Company is headquartered in Vancouver, British Columbia. It cultivates, processes, and distributes cannabis and hemp in Arizona, California, Florida, Illinois, Massachusetts, and Michigan. More information is available at http://RedWhiteBloom.com

The Scotts Miracle-Gro Company (NYSE: SMG)

The Scotts Miracle-Gro Company was founded in 1868 and is headquartered in Marysville, Ohio. It manufactures, markets, and sells consumer lawn and garden products in the United States and internationally. The company operates through three segments: U.S. Consumer, Hawthorne, and Other. It offers lawn care products, such as lawn fertilizers, grass seed products, spreaders, other durable products, and outdoor cleaners, as well as lawn-related weed, pest, and disease control products.

The company also provides gardening and landscape products, including water-soluble and continuous-release plant foods, potting mixes and garden soils, mulch and decorative groundcover products, plant-related pest and disease control products, organic garden products, and lives goods and seeding solutions. In addition, it offers hydroponic products that help users to grow plants, flowers, and vegetables using little or no soil; lighting systems and components for use in hydroponic and indoor gardening applications; and insect, rodent, and weed control products for home areas.

The company offers its products under the Scotts, Turf Builder, EZ Seed, PatchMaster, Thick'R Lawn, GrubEx, EdgeGuard, Handy Green II, Miracle-Gro, LiquaFeed, Osmocote, Shake Â'N Feed, Hyponex, Earthgro, SuperSoil, Fafard, Nature Scapes, Ortho, Miracle-Gro Performance Organics, Miracle-Gro Organic Choice, Whitney Farms, EcoScraps, Mother Earth, Botanicare, Hydroponics, Vermicrop, Gavita, Agrolux, Can-Filters, Sun System, Gro Pro, Hurricane, AeroGarden, Titan, Tomcat, Ortho Weed B Gon, Roundup, Groundclear, and Alchemist brands. It serves home centers, mass merchandisers, warehouse clubs, large hardware chains, independent hardware stores, nurseries, garden centers, e-commerce platforms, and food and drug stores, as well as indoor gardening and hydroponic distributors, retailers, and growers through a direct sales force, and network of brokers and distributors. More information is available at http://scottsmiraclegro.com

Silver Spike Acquisition Corp. (NASDAQ: MAPS)

Silver Spike is a blank check company incorporated as a Cayman Islands exempted company on June 7, 2019. In August 2019, it successfully launched a US$ 250 million NASDAQ-listed SPAC, Silver Spike Acquisition Corp., which was underwritten by Credit Suisse. SSPK focuses on investing in businesses in the plant-based industry that are compliant with all applicable laws and regulations within the jurisdictions in which they are located or operate, including the U.S. Controlled Substances Act. In December 2020, SSPK announced a merger agreement with WM Holdings, operator of Weedmaps, an online listings marketplace for cannabis consumers and a provider of software and other technology solutions for cannabis retailers and brands. That transaction was consummated on June 16, 2021 via Spike's combination with WM Holding Company, LLC, which is the operator of Weedmaps. After that transaction, the NASDAQ stock symbol SSPK was changed to MAPS. More information is available at https://www.silverspikecap.com

SLANG Worldwide Inc. (OTC: SLGWF) (CSE: SLNG)

SLANG was incorporated in 2017 and is headquartered in Toronto, Canada. The company was formerly known as Fire Cannabis Inc. and changed its name to SLANG Worldwide Inc. in November 2018. SLANG operates as a cannabis consumer packaged goods company worldwide. It owns, licenses, and/or markets 11 brands which serve flower, inhalable concentrates, and ingestibles, including edibles and pressed pills. More information is available at http://slangww.com

Stable Road Acquisition Corporation (NASDAQ: SRAC)

Stable Road Acquisition Corp. with headquarters in Venice, California filed an S-1 with the SEC on October 29, 2029 as a newly organized blank check company (SPAC) formed for the purpose of effecting a merger, capital stock exchange, asset acquisition, stock purchase, reorganization or similar business combination with one or more businesses, which we refer to as our initial business combination. It stated that while it had not selected any target it intended to focus its search on companies in the cannabis industry.

Its initial public offering (IPO) consisted of 15 million units at an offering price of $10.00. Each unit consisted of one share of our Class A common stock and one-half of one redeemable warrant. Only whole warrants were exercisable and allowed the purchase of one share of Class A common stock at a price of $11.50 per share. The underwriters were given an option to acquire an additional 2,250,000 units at the $10 offering price, which they exercised. That brought the gross proceeds of the IPO to $172.5 million.

Purchasers of IPO units were given the opportunity to redeem all or a portion of their shares of our Class A common stock upon the completion of Stable Road's initial business combination. If Stable Road did not complete its qualifying transaction within 18 months from the closing of its IPO, it stated it would redeem 100% of the public shares for cash. Its IPO closed on November 13, 2019. More information is available at http://stableroadcapital.com

Stem Holdings Inc. (OTC: STMH) (CSE: STEM)

Stem Holdings Inc. was founded in 2016 and is headquartered in Boca Raton, Florida. It is an omnichannel, vertically-integrated cannabis branded products and technology company with cultivation, processing, extraction, retail, distribution, and delivery-as-a-service (DaaS) operations throughout the United States. It is involved in manufacture, possession, use, sale, distribution, and branding of cannabis and cannabis-infused products under the laws of the states of Oregon, Nevada, California, Massachusetts, and Oklahoma. As of December 30, 2020, the company had ownership interests in 22 state issued cannabis and hemp licenses, including 10 licenses for cannabis cultivation; 4 licenses for cannabis processing; 1 license for cannabis wholesale distribution; 1 license for hemp production and processing; 5 cannabis dispensary licenses; and 1 license that permits both dispensary and cultivation activities.

Stem's family of brands includes TJ's Gardens™, TravisxJames™, and Yerba Buena™ flower and extracts; Cannavore™ edible confections; Doseology™, a CBD mass-market brand launching in 2021; as well as DaaS brands Budee™ and Ganjarunner™ through the acquisition of Driven Deliveries. Budee™ and Ganjarunner™ e-commerce platforms provide direct-to consumer proprietary logistics and an omnichannel UX (user experience)/CX (customer experience). More information is available at http://stemholdings.com

Subversive Capital Acquisition Corp.

Subversive Capital Acquisition Corp. was established as a SPAC under the laws of British Columbia for the purpose of effecting, directly or indirectly, a qualifying transaction within a specified period of time. Its goal is to consolidate the well-established California cannabis market by investing in minority-owned cannabis companies as well as companies with large-scale cultivation and a history of strong distribution. It raised $575 million in its IPO, which set a record for cannabis SPACs. After its qualifying transaction, subversive became known as The Parent Company or TPCO. More information is available at https://www.theparent.co

TerrAscend Corp. (OTC: TRSSF) (CSE: TER)

TerrAscend was incorporated in 2017 and is based in Mississauga, Canada. It cultivates, processes, and sells medical and adult use cannabis in Canada, California, Maryland, New Jersey, and Pennsylvania. It produces and distributes hemp-derived wellness products to retail locations; and manufactures cannabis infused artisan edibles. The company also operates retail dispensaries under the Apothecarium brand name.. The Company owns several synergistic businesses and brands, including The Apothecarium, Ilera Healthcare, Kind Tree, Prism, State Flower, Valhalla Confections, and Arise Bioscience Inc. More information is available at http://terrascend.com

Tilray (NASDAQ: TLRY)

Tilray is the second largest Canadian cannabis company as measured by its market capitalization. It is headquartered in Leamington, Canada. On April 30, 2021 Aphria Inc. and Tilray Inc. merged and Aphria shares were converted into Tilray shares. The company engages in the research, cultivation, production, and distribution of medical cannabis and cannabinoids on a global basis. It has operations in Australia, Canada, Europe, Latin America, and the United States. Tilray's production platform supports over 20 brands in over 20 countries, including comprehensive cannabis offerings, hempbased foods, and alcoholic beverages. It offers medical cannabis in extracts and dried flower forms; and cannabis extracts, including purified oil drops and capsules. The company supplies cannabis extract products to patients, physicians, pharmacies, hospitals, governments, and researchers. More information is available at http://Tilray.com

TILT Holdings (OTC: TLLTF) (CSE: TILT)

TILT was founded in 2017 and is headquartered in Phoenix, Arizona. It services brands and cannabis retailers across 36 states in the U.S., as well as Canada, European Union, Israel, Mexico, and South America. TILT's core businesses include Jupiter Research LLC, a wholly-owned subsidiary that designs and manufactures vaporization products.

TILT also cultivates, processes, and distributes cannabis via Commonwealth Alternative Care, Inc. in Massachusetts, Standard Farms LLC in Pennsylvania, and Standard Farms Ohio, LLC in Ohio. It offers a range of products and services across the cannabis industry; and logistic operations and software solutions throughout the cannabis supply chain. More information is available at http://tiltholding.com

TPCO Holding Corp. (OTC: GRAMF) (NEO: GRAM.U)

The Parent Company, known as TPCO Holding Corp., was founded in 2019 and is headquartered in San Jose, California. TPCO was formerly known as Subversive Capital Acquisition Corporation, which was a SPAC, until it qualifying transaction occurred in January 2021. TPCO cultivates, extracts, manufactures, distributes, retails, and delivers cannabis in California. The company offers approximately 17 owned and licensed brands offering 250 stock keeping units across 20 form-factors, such as jarred and bagged whole flower, pre-rolls, infused pre-rolls, bulk extracts, vaporizer cartridges, ready-to-use vapes, concentrates, gummies, chocolate, beverages, capsules, tinctures, lozenges, topicals, bath bombs, and body care products. It also offers its products under the Monogram, Caliva, Mind Your Head, Mirayo by Santana, Soul Spring, and other brands, as well as through Caliva.com, a direct-to-consumer e-commerce platform. TPCO a/k/a The Parent Company has teamed-up with Shawn "JAY-Z" Carter, ROC NATION, direct-to-consumer platform CALIVA, and cannabis manufacturer, LEFT COAST VENTURES, to form a cannabis coalition. TPCO named Carter its Chief Visionary Officer. More information is available at http://theparent.co

Trulieve (OTC: TCNNF) (CSE: TRUL)

Trulieve was the first company to open a licensed medical marijuana dispensary in Florida. It is headquartered in Quincy, Florida and is among the largest cannabis companies in the United States as measured by market capitalization. Trulieve cultivates, processes, and distributes its cannabis products in California, Connecticut, Florida, Massachusetts, Pennsylvania, and West Virginia.

It produces approximately 550 stock keeping units "SKUs" including flower, edibles, vaporizer cartridges, concentrates, topicals, capsules, tinctures, dissolvable powders, and nasal sprays. More information is available at http://trulieve.com

Tuatara Capital Acquisition Corp. (NASDAQ: TCACU)

Tuatara is a special purpose acquisition company (SPAC) based in New York City. It intends to capitalize on opportunities in the cannabis industry. Its business strategy is to identify and complete one or more business combinations with a target operating in the cannabis industry that is compliant with all applicable laws and regulations within the jurisdictions in which it is located or operates. It seeks targets that can materially grow revenue and earnings both organically and inorganically. More information is available at http://tuataraspac.com

Tuscan Holdings Corp II (NASDAQ: THCA)

Tuscan Holdings Corp. II is a blank check company (SPAC) formed for the purpose of entering into a merger, share exchange, asset acquisition, stock purchase, recapitalization, reorganization or other similar business combination with one or more businesses or entities in a target business. Tuscan's efforts to identify a prospective target business are not limited to a particular industry or geographic region although it intends to focus its search for target businesses in the cannabis industry. https://www.sec.gov/Archives/edgar/data/1773087/000121390019012692/f424b40719_tuscanholdcorpii.htm

Verano Holdings Corporation (OTC: VRNOF) (CSE: VRNO)

Verano Holdings Corp. was founded in 2017 and is headquartered in Chicago, Illinois. It is a vertically-integrated, multi-state cannabis operator in the United States. Verano produces cannabis products sold under its consumer brands: Verano, Avexia, Encore, and MÜV™. The Company's portfolio encompasses 14 U.S. States, with active operations in 11, which includes nine production facilities comprising approximately 770,000 square feet of cultivation. Verano designs, builds, and operates dispensaries under retail brands Zen Leaf™ and MÜV™. More information is available at http://verano.com

Vext Science, Inc. (OTC: VEXTF) (CSE: VEXT)

The company was formerly known as Vapen MJ Ventures Corporation and changed its name to Vext Science, Inc. in November 2019. Vext Science, Inc. was incorporated in 2015. Its U.S. headquarters is in Phoenix and its legal address is in Vancouver, British Columbia. Vext Science, Inc., through its subsidiaries, operates as an integrated agricultural technology, services, and property management company in the cannabis industry in the United States. The company is involved in the cultivation, extraction, manufacture, and sale of THC and CBD cartridges, concentrates, and edibles. It also engages in the retail dispensary activities; and wholesale distribution of cannabis THC and hemp CBD products under the Vapen and Pure Touch Botanicals brands. In addition, the company offers Vapen clear infused products, THC chocolate bars, THC syrup, THC snacks, candies, and gummies under Vapen Kitchens brand. More information is available at http://www.vextscience.com

Vibe Growth Corporation (OTC: VBSCF) (CSE: VIBE)

Vibe is headquartered in Sacramento, California. It is a vertically integrated cannabis organization that operates retail dispensaries; cannabis greenhouse cultivation; premium indoor cultivation; commercial distribution and transportation; e-commerce and home delivery; and the manufacturing of Hype Cannabis Co. marijuana products. The Company operates retail and e-commerce under its Vibe by California brand. More information is available at http://www.vibebycalifornia.com

WM Holding Company (NASDAQ: MAPS)

WM Holding Company is a cannabis technology company that operates the online U.S. platform Weedmaps where users find and rate marijuana sellers. The Irvine, California based company was founded in 2008 and offers a cloud operating system for cannabis retailers as well as hosting a review and ratings platform for sellers. The company became publicly held at a $1.5 billion valuation on June 16, 2021 when it was combined with Silver Spike Acquisition Corp. More information is available at https://www.silverspikecap.com

XS Financial Inc. (OTC: XSHLF) (CSE: XSF)

XS Financial Inc. was incorporated in 2009 and is based in Los Angeles, California. The company was formerly known as Xtraction Services Holdings Corp. and changed its name to XS Financial Inc. in June 2020. XS Financial Inc., a specialty finance company, provides equipment leasing solutions in the United States. It offers equipment-specific leasing, sale-leasebacks, and purchasing solutions. The company provides equipment procurement services. It serves owner/operators of cannabis and hemp companies, including cultivators, oil processors, manufacturers, and testing laboratories. More information is available at https://www.xsfinancial.com

Zynerba Pharmaceuticals (NASDAQ: ZYNE)

Zynerba Pharmaceuticals, Inc., together with its subsidiary, Zynerba Pharmaceuticals Pty Ltd, the is a clinical stage specialty pharmaceutical company focused on the development of pharmaceutically-produced transdermal cannabinoid therapies for rare and near-rare neuropsychiatric disorders, including Fragile X syndrome, autism spectrum disorder, 22q11.2 deletion syndrome, and a heterogeneous group of rare and ultra-rare epilepsies known as developmental and epileptic encephalopathies.

The Company has incurred losses and negative cash flows from operations since inception, has no sales revenue, and has an accumulated deficit of $210.1 million as of March 31, 2021. The Company anticipates incurring additional losses until such time, if ever, that it can generate significant revenue from its product candidates currently in development. The Company's primary source of liquidity has been the issuance of equity securities. More information is available at https://zynerba.com

APPENDIX B

GLOSSARY

Accumulated Deficit
- Net loss incurred by a company since its formation

Adjusted Net Income Before Taxes
- Income before taxes from statement of profits and losses excluding the impact of biologicals

Adjusted Net Operating Income
- Total revenue after discounts and taxes minus operating expenses excluding the impact of biologicals

AUM
- Dollar amount of assets under management

Basis Point
- 1% equals 100 basis points; therefore, 1 basis point equals 1/100th of 1 percent

Book Value
- Shareholders' Equity from balance sheet

CAGR
- Compound annual growth rate

CAPEX
- Capital expenditures on plant and equipment

EBITDA
- Net income before interest expense, taxes, depreciation and amortization

ETF
- Exchange traded fund, composed of a portfolio of securities. Shares of an ETF can be bought and sold through the day on stock exchanges

Free Cash Flow
- Net cash flow provided by operations minus increase (or plus decrease) in current income taxes payable

Gross Profit
- Total revenue after discounts and taxes minus cost of goods sold

ITM
- In-the-money refers to a security that can be converted into another security at a profit

Limit Order
- An order to buy a specified number of shares at or below a specified price or an order to sell a specified number of shares at or above a specified price

Lock-Up Period
- The period of time during which people covered by lock up agreements cannot sell their stock

NAV
- The total market value of all shares in an ETF divided by the number of shares outstanding

NIAT
- Net income after taxes

NM
- Not meaningful. The number could not be calculated, because the numerator or denominator was negative

Operating Expenses
- Total operating expenses shown on statement of profits and losses.

Operating Cash Flow
- Net cash provided by or used in operating activities on statement of cash flows

PE Ratio
- Net income after tax attributable to one share of company stock divided by price of a share

PEG Ratio
- PE Ratio divided by annualized growth rate in net income per share

REIT
- A real estate investment trust, which is a company that invests in real estate and pays out at least 90% of its income so it is not taxable

ROE
- Return on equity, which equals net income after taxes divided by shareholders' equity

RTO
- Reverse takeover, which is the way most cannabis companies were formed in Canada

SPAC
- Special purpose acquisition company established by people to enrich themselves

Sequential Change
- Change from immediately prior quarter

TAM
- Total addressable market, which usually refers to the number of potential customers in a particular market

Tangible Book Value
- Shareholder equity minus goodwill and intangible assets

Tax Adjusted Operating Cash Flow
- Net cash flow provided by operations minus increase (or plus decrease) in current taxes payable

Up-listing
- When a company moves its shares from trading on the OTC market to the NYSE or NASDAQ

YOY
- Year-over-year change from same quarter last year

APPENDIX C

BIBLIOGRAPHY

_____. Baker, James V. "Impact of 280e On Cannabis Net Income," https://seekingalpha.com/article/4435492-impact-of-280e-on-cannabis-company-net-income, June 18, 2021.

_____. "Cronos Sets Its Sights On USA," https://seekingalpha.com/article/4434927-Cronos-sets-its-sights-on-usa, June 15, 2021.

_____. "Did You Know or Have Suspicions About the Harvest Health Deal," https://seekingalpha.com/article/4427406-did-you-know-or-have-suspicions-about-the-harvest-deal, May 11, 2021.

_____. "Liberty Health Sciences Shareholders Offer to Support Other Bidders," https://seekingalpha.com/article/4399108-liberty-health-sciences-shareholders-offer-to-support-bidders, January 15, 2021.

_____. "Twins Comparison Screams Liberty Health Sciences Shareholders Deserve More Compensation," https://seekingalpha.com/article/4398343-twins-comparison-screams-liberty-health-sciences-shareholders-deserve-compensation, January 11, 2021.

_____. "U.S. Cannabis Companies Set to Soar," https://seekingalpha.com/article/4398301-u-s-cannabis-companies-set-to-soar, January 11, 2021.

_____. "Liberty Health Sciences Shareholders Want Higher Price," https://seekingalpha.com/article/4396686-liberty-health-sciences-shareholders-want-higher-price, December 30, 2020.

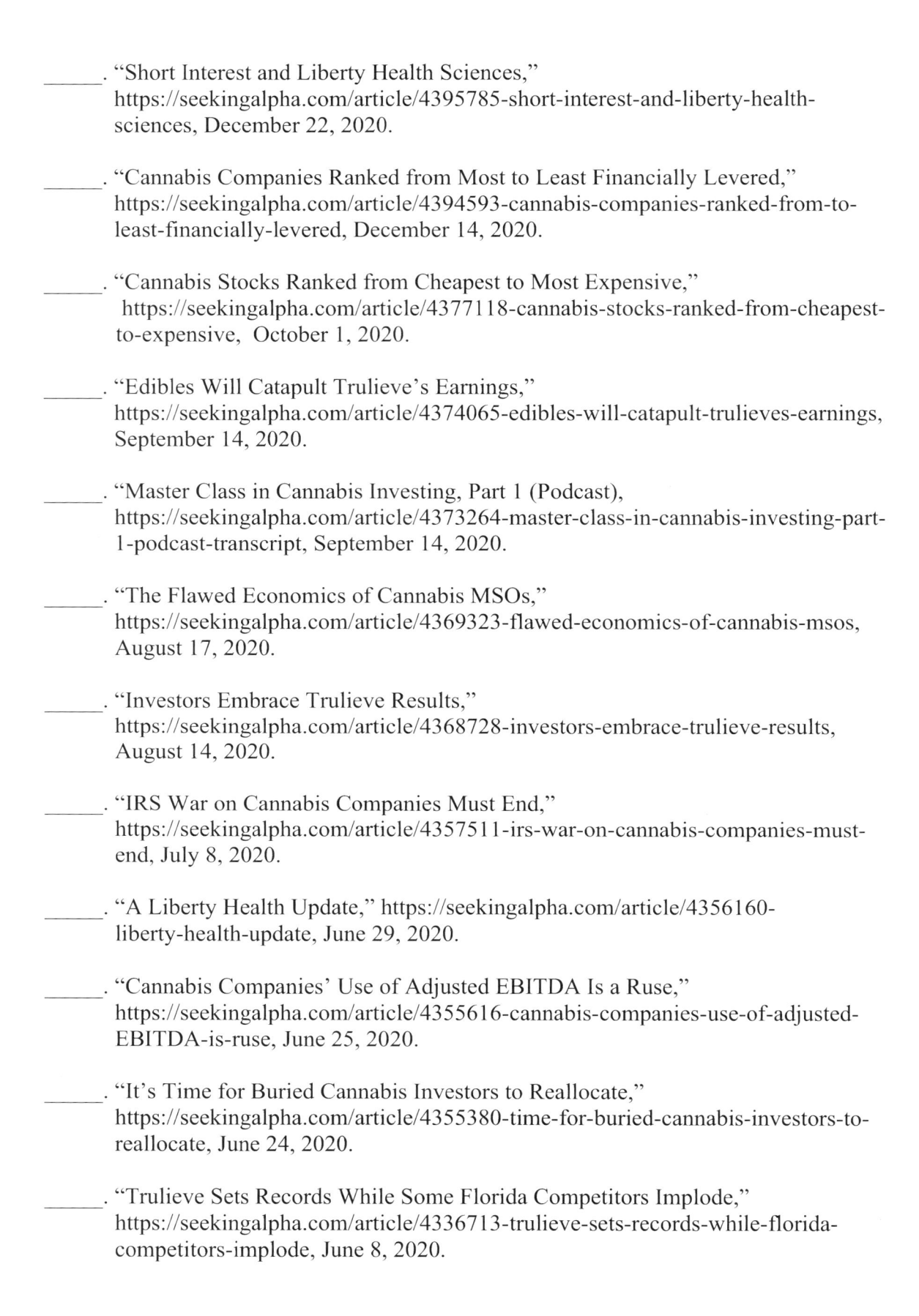

_____. "Short Interest and Liberty Health Sciences," https://seekingalpha.com/article/4395785-short-interest-and-liberty-health-sciences, December 22, 2020.

_____. "Cannabis Companies Ranked from Most to Least Financially Levered," https://seekingalpha.com/article/4394593-cannabis-companies-ranked-from-to-least-financially-levered, December 14, 2020.

_____. "Cannabis Stocks Ranked from Cheapest to Most Expensive," https://seekingalpha.com/article/4377118-cannabis-stocks-ranked-from-cheapest-to-expensive, October 1, 2020.

_____. "Edibles Will Catapult Trulieve's Earnings," https://seekingalpha.com/article/4374065-edibles-will-catapult-trulieves-earnings, September 14, 2020.

_____. "Master Class in Cannabis Investing, Part 1 (Podcast), https://seekingalpha.com/article/4373264-master-class-in-cannabis-investing-part-1-podcast-transcript, September 14, 2020.

_____. "The Flawed Economics of Cannabis MSOs," https://seekingalpha.com/article/4369323-flawed-economics-of-cannabis-msos, August 17, 2020.

_____. "Investors Embrace Trulieve Results," https://seekingalpha.com/article/4368728-investors-embrace-trulieve-results, August 14, 2020.

_____. "IRS War on Cannabis Companies Must End," https://seekingalpha.com/article/4357511-irs-war-on-cannabis-companies-must-end, July 8, 2020.

_____. "A Liberty Health Update," https://seekingalpha.com/article/4356160-liberty-health-update, June 29, 2020.

_____. "Cannabis Companies' Use of Adjusted EBITDA Is a Ruse," https://seekingalpha.com/article/4355616-cannabis-companies-use-of-adjusted-EBITDA-is-ruse, June 25, 2020.

_____. "It's Time for Buried Cannabis Investors to Reallocate," https://seekingalpha.com/article/4355380-time-for-buried-cannabis-investors-to-reallocate, June 24, 2020.

_____. "Trulieve Sets Records While Some Florida Competitors Implode," https://seekingalpha.com/article/4336713-trulieve-sets-records-while-florida-competitors-implode, June 8, 2020.

_____. "Liberty Health Sciences Is a Hidden Gem," https://seekingalpha.com/article/4330943-liberty-health-sciences-is-hidden-gem, March 10, 2020.

_____. "Trulieve Continues to Profitably Dominate Florida's Marijuana Industry, https://seekingalpha.com/article/4329727-trulieve-continues-to-profitably-dominate-floridas-marijuana-industry, March 4, 2020.

_____. "Where Can Stocks Find Support?" https://seekingalpha.com/instablog/55954-james-v-baker/5415273-where-can-stocks-find-support, March 1, 2020.

_____. "Largest Cannabis MSOs Are Sending SOS Signals," https://seekingalpha.com/article/4300355-largest-cannabis-msos-are-sending-sos-signals, October 30, 2019.

_____. "Cannabis Investors' Losses Soar on First Anniversary Of Recreational Use in Canada, https://seekingalpha.com/article/4298630-cannabis-investors-losses-soar-on-first-anniversary-of-recreational-use-in-canada, October 24, 2019.

_____. "An Update on The Florida Medical Marijuana Market," https://seekingalpha.com/article/4296454-update-on-florida-medical-marijuana-market, October 14, 2019.

_____. "Florida Seed-To-Sale License System Ruled Unconstitutional," https://seekingalpha.com/article/4275693-florida-seed-to-sale-license-system-ruled-unconstitutional, July 18, 2019.

_____. "Trulieve Cannabis Has Lost Its Luster," https://seekingalpha.com/article/4254174-trulieve-cannabis-lost-luster, April 12, 2019.

_____. "MedMen Hovers on The Brink as Its Co-Founders Learn on The Job," https://seekingalpha.com/article/4246193-medmen-hovers-on-brink-co-founders-learn-on-job, March 4, 2019.

_____. "Will Harvest Health & Recreation Become the Most Valuable Cannabis Company on Earth," https://seekingalpha.com/article/4244492-will-harvest-health-and-recreation-become-valuable-cannabis-company-earth, February 26, 2019.

_____. "Has Canopy Growth Morphed into A Target?" https://seekingalpha.com/article/4241386-canopy-growth-morphed-target, February 15, 2019.

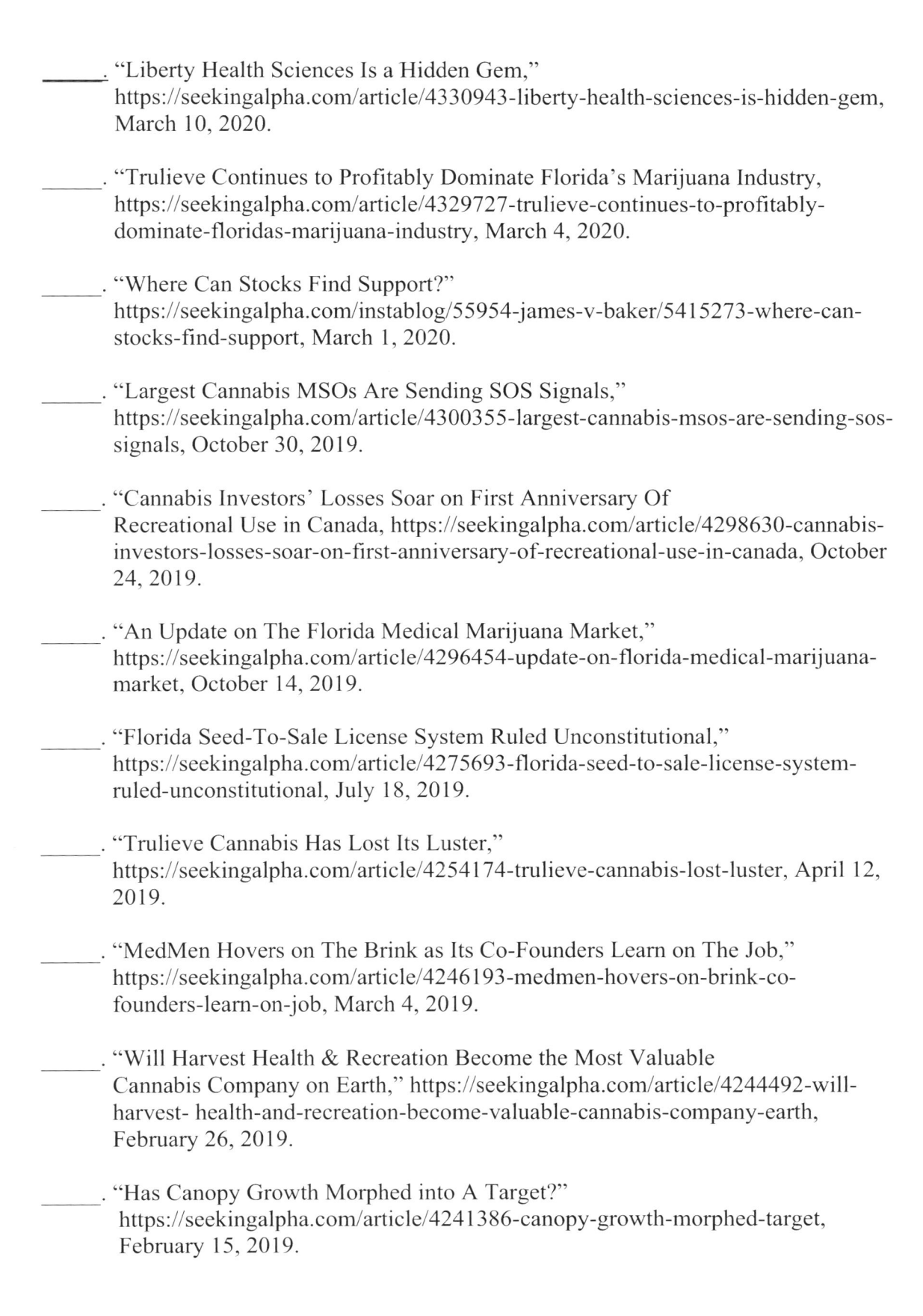

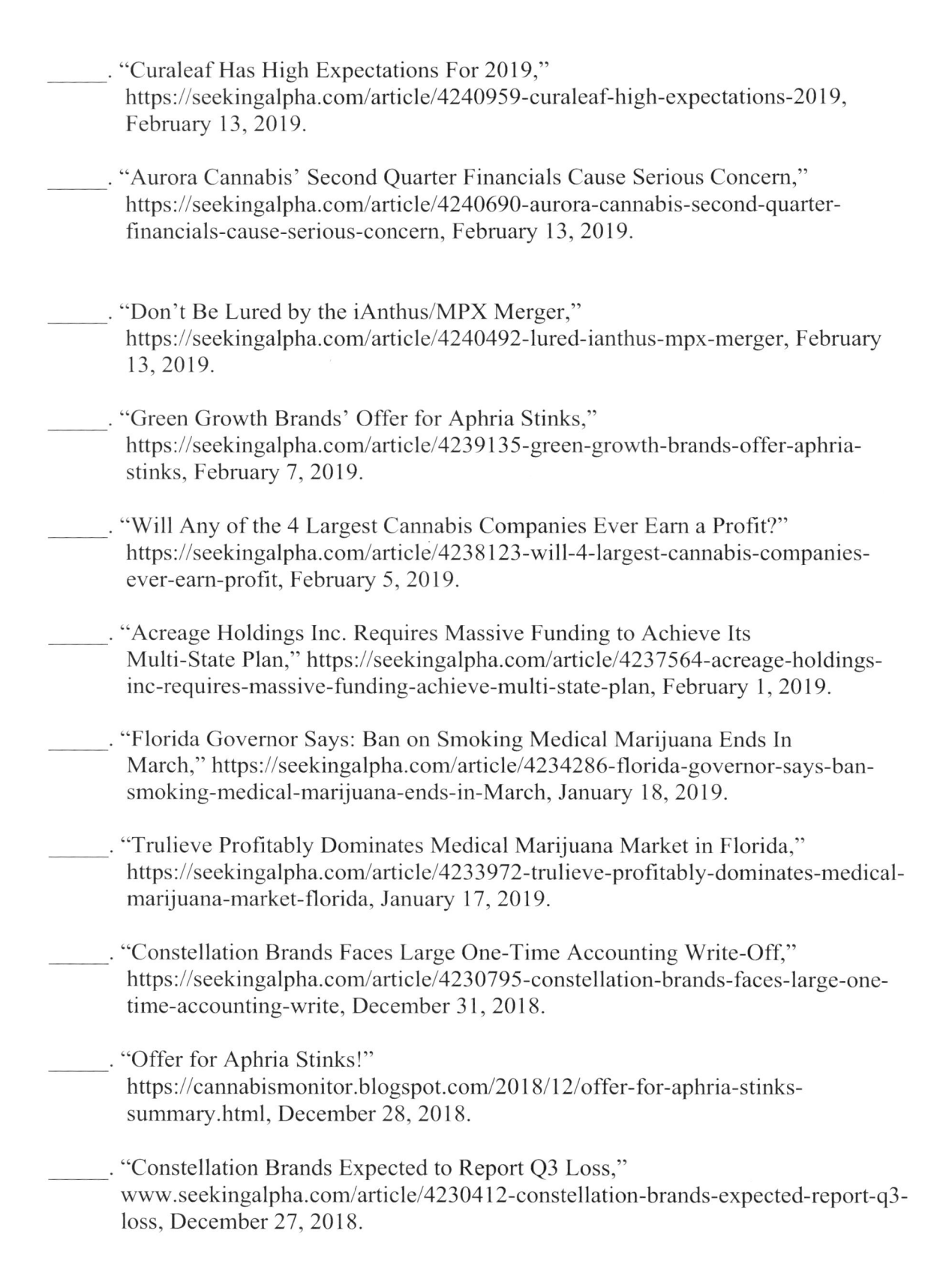

_____. "Curaleaf Has High Expectations For 2019," https://seekingalpha.com/article/4240959-curaleaf-high-expectations-2019, February 13, 2019.

_____. "Aurora Cannabis' Second Quarter Financials Cause Serious Concern," https://seekingalpha.com/article/4240690-aurora-cannabis-second-quarter-financials-cause-serious-concern, February 13, 2019.

_____. "Don't Be Lured by the iAnthus/MPX Merger," https://seekingalpha.com/article/4240492-lured-ianthus-mpx-merger, February 13, 2019.

_____. "Green Growth Brands' Offer for Aphria Stinks," https://seekingalpha.com/article/4239135-green-growth-brands-offer-aphria-stinks, February 7, 2019.

_____. "Will Any of the 4 Largest Cannabis Companies Ever Earn a Profit?" https://seekingalpha.com/article/4238123-will-4-largest-cannabis-companies-ever-earn-profit, February 5, 2019.

_____. "Acreage Holdings Inc. Requires Massive Funding to Achieve Its Multi-State Plan," https://seekingalpha.com/article/4237564-acreage-holdings-inc-requires-massive-funding-achieve-multi-state-plan, February 1, 2019.

_____. "Florida Governor Says: Ban on Smoking Medical Marijuana Ends In March," https://seekingalpha.com/article/4234286-florida-governor-says-ban-smoking-medical-marijuana-ends-in-March, January 18, 2019.

_____. "Trulieve Profitably Dominates Medical Marijuana Market in Florida," https://seekingalpha.com/article/4233972-trulieve-profitably-dominates-medical-marijuana-market-florida, January 17, 2019.

_____. "Constellation Brands Faces Large One-Time Accounting Write-Off," https://seekingalpha.com/article/4230795-constellation-brands-faces-large-one-time-accounting-write, December 31, 2018.

_____. "Offer for Aphria Stinks!" https://cannabismonitor.blogspot.com/2018/12/offer-for-aphria-stinks-summary.html, December 28, 2018.

_____. "Constellation Brands Expected to Report Q3 Loss," www.seekingalpha.com/article/4230412-constellation-brands-expected-report-q3-loss, December 27, 2018.